GACE

Paraprofessional Practice Questions

I0878854

Mometrix
TEST PREPARATION

DEAR FUTURE EXAM SUCCESS STORY

First of all, **THANK YOU** for purchasing Mometrix study materials!

Second, congratulations! You are one of the few determined test-takers who are committed to doing whatever it takes to excel on your exam. **You have come to the right place.** We developed these practice tests with one goal in mind: to deliver you the best possible approximation of the questions you will see on test day.

Standardized testing is one of the biggest obstacles on your road to success, which only increases the importance of doing well in the high-pressure, high-stakes environment of test day. Your results on this test could have a significant impact on your future, and these practice tests will give you the repetitions you need to build your familiarity and confidence with the test content and format to help you achieve your full potential on test day.

Your success is our success

We would love to hear from you! If you would like to share the story of your exam success or if you have any questions or comments in regard to our products, please contact us at **800-673-8175** or **support@mometrix.com**.

Thanks again for your business and we wish you continued success!

Sincerely,
The Mometrix Test Preparation Team

TABLE OF CONTENTS

Practice Test #1

Reading

Refer to the following for questions 1–3:

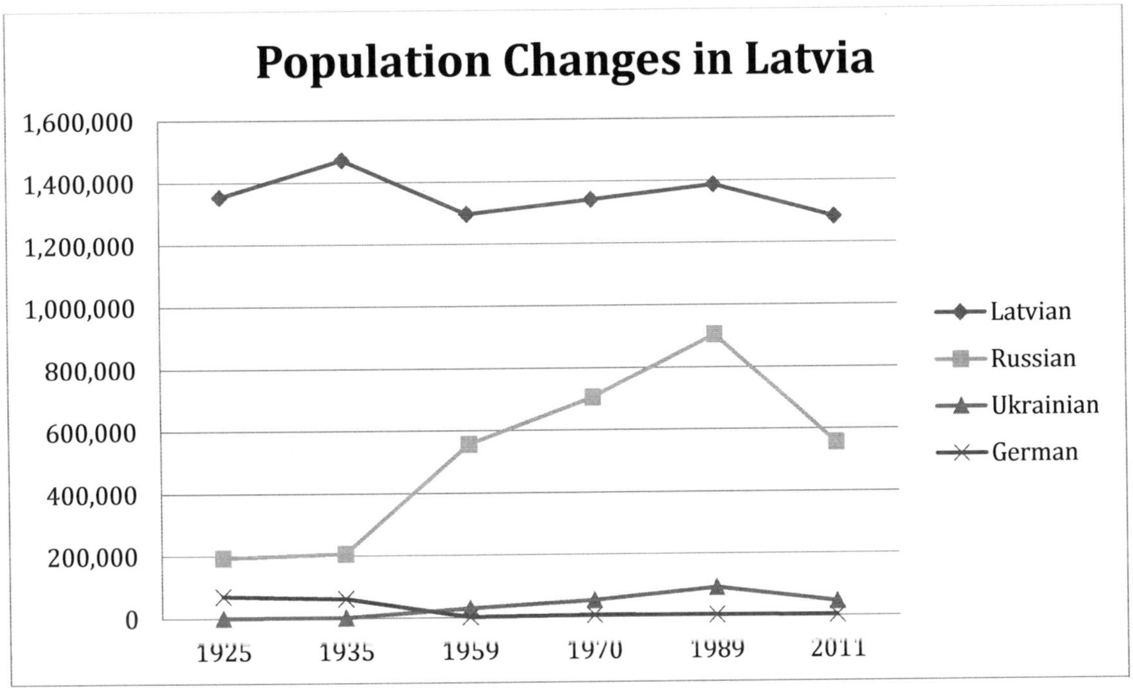

1. Between 1925 and 1991, Latvia was part of the Soviet Union. Since 1991, the population of which ethnic group in Latvia appears to have decreased the most?

a. Latvian
b. Russian
c. Ukrainian
d. German

2. After World War II ended in 1945, large numbers of non-Latvian workers entered the country, primarily to work at construction jobs. Among these non-Latvian ethnic groups, the increase in workers represented a population percentage shift of less than one percent before 1945 to more than three percent by the time of the Soviet Union's collapse. Which ethnic group shown on the chart best represents this shift?

a. Latvian
b. Russian
c. Ukrainian
d. German

3. Which ethnic group's population had the least change after the end of World War II?

a. Latvian
b. Russian
c. Ukrainian
d. German

Refer to the following for questions 4–6:

Although technological tools like polygraph tests, psychological theories, and interrogation techniques have resulted in slightly greater accuracy for law enforcement agents catching liars, it is still important to understand the nature of lies and check unfounded assumptions that can lead to unquestioning acceptance of false statements. Because intentional deception is one of the biggest obstacles to a successful criminal investigation, developing the ability to separate dubious or outright false statements from true ones has to be one of the main goals of every police officer and law enforcement investigator. In addition, an officer must be able to quickly sort out the possible repercussions of a false statement and the ways it can affect the rest of an investigation, should one slip by police screening. This is the only way to punish the guilty, exonerate the innocent, and do the most possible good in preventing future crimes.

The most difficult lie to catch is the half-truth. Half-truths are distortions constructed by using a seed of truth as a way to sprout a more convincing lie. A half-truth may incorporate intentional exaggeration or understatement, lies of omission, false implications, or outright lies mixed in with actual facts. Half-truths that slip past the detectives investigating a case are classified as either "smoke" lies or "mirror" lies. Smoke refers to half-truths that slow down an investigation by casting doubt on otherwise promising leads or angles of investigation. Mirrors are lies that manage to send the detective off in the wrong direction altogether, usually by linking a fact to a false supposition.

Most other lies are overt and intentional. Usually, they are told as a way for a suspect or witness to protect himself or his friends or, more rarely, to cast suspicion on a rival. In some cases, these sorts of lies can be compounded by overzealous or corrupt police who want to earn a conviction of a supposed perpetrator at any cost. Particularly in high-profile cases with gruesome details, this sort of lie results in more false convictions than any other type of distortion.

4. Which statement most accurately conveys the essay's main idea?

a. New police techniques have been ineffective at helping investigators catch liars.
b. The worst lies aren't outright lies; they're sneaky half-truths.
c. People in law enforcement need to be able to recognize lies to be effective and just.
d. There are only two primary types of lies.

5. The essay's writer would be most likely to say that a police officer's ability to recognize both lies and half-truths is:

a. Indispensable in a criminal investigation
b. Difficult because of the sophistication of some liars
c. The most important tool that law enforcement has
d. Crucial, but beyond the abilities of most officers

6. According to the essay, "smoke":

a. Is the most frequently told type of half-truth
b. Never contains outright lies mixed in with truth
c. Can slow down an investigation
d. Sends detectives off in the wrong direction altogether

Refer to the following for questions 7–9:

Jo's face was a study next day, for the secret rather weighed upon her, and she found it hard not to look mysterious and important. Meg observed it, but did not trouble herself to make inquiries, for she had learned that the best way to manage Jo was by the law of contraries, so she felt sure of being told everything if she did not ask. She was rather surprised, therefore, when the silence remained unbroken, and Jo assumed a patronizing air, which decidedly aggravated Meg, who in turn assumed an air of dignified reserve and devoted herself to her mother. This left Jo to her own devices, for Mrs. March had taken her place as nurse, and bade her rest, exercise, and amuse herself after her long confinement. Amy being gone, Laurie was her only refuge, and much as she enjoyed his society, she rather dreaded him just then, for he was an incorrigible tease, and she feared he would coax the secret from her.

(*Little Women* by Louisa May Alcott)

7. From what point of view is this passage written?

a. First person
b. Second person
c. Third person
d. Fourth person

8. The phrase *was a study* implies that:

a. Jo looked jubilant.
b. Jo looked secretive.
c. Jo looked disheveled.
d. Jo looked angry.

9. What can you infer about Laurie?

a. He was stoic.
b. He was taciturn.
c. He was unruly.
d. He was uncanny.

Refer to the following for questions 10–12:

Lisa Grant: "Schools should make students wear uniforms. Everyone would look the same. Students would be able to respect each other based on their ideas and character because they would no longer be judged by their appearance."

Vivian Harris: "Students should not have to wear uniforms. Clothing is an important part of self-expression. Taking away that method of expression is suppressing that student's rights."

10. What is one idea that the students above seem to agree on, based on their statements?

a. Students should be allowed to express themselves through apparel.
b. Schools should give students a certain amount of respect.
c. Students should focus more on school than on appearance.
d. Schools would violate students' basic rights by enforcing a dress code.

11. Which of the following statements could NOT provide support for BOTH arguments?

a. A number of local school districts have recently implemented dress codes.
b. School administrators have been in talks with parents over the issue of uniforms.
c. Students have reported that school uniforms are costly and typically ill-fitting.
d. Several groups of students have been organized to discuss uniform dress codes.

12. Which of the following would be an effective primary source to support Vivian Harris's argument?

a. A study showing that fewer students are bullied at schools that require uniforms
b. An article describing the negative effects of uniforms in American schools
c. An interview with a local principal who regrets implementing uniform requirements
d. A persuasive essay written by Vivian that includes statistics and quotes from psychological studies and other students that support her position

Refer to the following for questions 13–21:

EARLY POLITICAL PARTIES

The United States has always been a pluralistic society, meaning it has always embraced many points of view and many groups with different identities. That is not to say that these groups have always seen eye to eye. The first political parties developed in the United States as a result of conflicting visions of the American identity. Many politicians believed that wealthy merchants and lawyers represented the country's true identity, but many others saw it in the farmers and workers who formed the country's economic base.

The event that brought this disagreement to the surface was the creation of the Bank of the United States in 1791. The bank set out to rid the country of the debts it had accumulated during the American Revolution. Until then, each state was responsible for its own debts. The Bank of the United States, however, wanted to assume these debts and pay them off itself. While many people considered this offer to be a good financial deal for the states, many states were uncomfortable with the arrangement because they saw it as a power play by the federal government. If a central bank had control over the finances of individual states, the people who owned the bank would profit from the states in the future. This concern was the basis of the disagreement: Who should have more power, the individual states or the central government?

The Democratic-Republican Party developed to protest the bank, but it came to represent a vision of America with power spread among states. The Federalist Party was established in defense of the bank, but its ultimate vision was of a strong central government that could help steer the United States toward a more competitive position in the world economy.

These different points of view—central government versus separate states—would not be resolved easily. These same disagreements fueled the tension that erupted into the Civil War over half a century later.

13. According to the passage, the word "pluralistic" most nearly means:

a. Divisive
b. Conservative
c. Tolerant
d. Liberty

14. What is the author's purpose in writing this passage?

a. To persuade the reader to accept the Federalist Party's point of view
b. To explain the disagreements between early American political parties
c. To explain the importance of a strong central government
d. To criticize the founders of the Bank of the United States

15. The word "competitive" is used in the passage to mean:

a. Inferior
b. Stronger
c. Partisan
d. Identity

16. In the last sentence of the first paragraph, the pronoun "it" refers to which of the following?

a. The country's identity
b. The future of the country
c. States' rights
d. A political party

17. Which of the following statements can be inferred from the second paragraph?

a. The formation of the Bank of the United States should not have created so much conflict.
b. Individual states believed that they should not have to share their profits with the central government.
c. The bank was attempting to swindle the states.
d. The states were not willing to listen to reason.

18. Which of the following statements best fits with the viewpoint of the Federalist Party?

a. The US should be a confederacy of individual states with equal power.
b. The government should not meddle in the affairs of states.
c. States should not have any rights.
d. The stronger the central government, the stronger the country.

19. Which of the following statements best fits with the viewpoint of the Democratic-Republican Party?

a. The federal government should not have too much power.
b. The Bank of the United States would never be able to repay the states' debts.
c. The states should not have too much power.
d. The constitution must be revised to give the government more power.

20. Which of the following statements can be inferred from the final paragraph?

a. The Civil War was fought between the Federalist and the Democratic-Republican Parties.
b. The different interests reflected by the first two political parties were not easily reconciled.
c. The Civil War could have been avoided if the Bank of the United States had not been created.
d. The Bank of the United States is a direct cause of the Civil War.

21. Which of the following best describes the main idea of the passage?

a. Political parties should emphasize areas of agreement instead of disagreement.
b. The earliest political parties in the US reflected conflicting interests.
c. The Federalist Party had a better plan for America's interests abroad.
d. The Bank of the United States was not a secure financial institution.

22. Which of the following instructional strategies would help students recognize the text structures of comparison and contrast or cause and effect in a history textbook?

a. defining the historical events occurring in a certain time period
b. showing students how to recognize signal words such as "similar to" or "instead of," which show these text structures
c. providing a timeline of the period of history being discussed
d. discussing the maps provided throughout the textbook

23. A history teacher discusses the structure of nonfiction texts by explaining the text structures of comparison and contrast, cause and effect, problem and solution, and chronological order. Which text structure do the following chapter titles from *A Textbook of the History of Architecture* represent?

CHAPTER I: PRIMITIVE AND PREHISTORIC ARCHITECTURE
CHAPTER X: .EARLY CHRISTIAN ARCHITECTURE
CHAPTER XIII: EARLY MEDIAEVAL ARCHITECTURE IN ITALY AND FRANCE
CHAPTER XX: EARLY RENAISSANCE ARCHITECTURE IN ITALY
CHAPTER XXVII: ARCHITECTURE IN THE UNITED STATES

a. comparison and contrast
b. cause and effect
c. chronological order
d. problem and solution

24. Students read an article in a magazine about codebreaking. This article showed how sending secret messages has evolved from wrapping parchment with secret messages around sticks to secret messages embedded in pictures and music on the Internet. This article showed the students that the technology of hidden messages has

a. remained the same through the years.
b. decreased through the years.
c. decreased in importance.
d. increased through the years.

25. After the eleventh-grade students read the World War II story of the brave German theologian Dietrich Bonhoeffer, a Lutheran minister who defied Hitler, the teacher had students explain their personal definitions of faith. This activity is likely to benefit students PRIMARILY by

a. introducing them to World War II.
b. teaching them about Germany.
c. involving them in the concept of faith.
d. providing a multicultural true story.

26. An English teacher asked her students to choose a novel and prepare an oral presentation on the language and style of their selection. Josh read from the first chapter of *The Adventures of Tom Sawyer* by Mark Twain, and gave his report.

"TOM!"

No answer.

"TOM!"

No answer.

"What's gone with that boy, I wonder? You TOM!"

No answer.

The old lady pulled her spectacles down and looked over them about the room; then she put them up and looked out under them. She seldom or never looked through them for so small a thing as a boy; they were her state pair, the pride of her heart, and they were built for "style," not service—she could have seen through a pair of stove-lids just as well. She looked perplexed for a moment, and then said, not fiercely, but still loud enough for the furniture to head:

"Well, I lay if I get hold of you I'll—"

She did not finish, for by this time she was bending down and punching under the bed with the broom, and so she needed breath to punctuate the punches with. She resurrected nothing but the cat.

The Adventures of Tom Sawyer by Mark Twain

Josh reported the word choices in the passage he read to be

a. colloquial.
b. abstract.
c. formal.
d. allusive.

27. John, who always felt like a failure when his teacher asked him to revise his work, was surprised when a visiting author talked about the extensive revisions in her books. What did he learn from the visiting author's presentation that helped him to better accept his teacher's request for revisions?

a. Revisions are rarely necessary.
b. Revisions are a normal process in writing.
c. Revisions show an inability to write a piece initially.
d. Revisions do not improve writing.

28. The English teacher read a passage from contemporary YA novel that shows a student's conflict with her mother. The main character, Beth, takes a stand against her mother's demand that she participate in art rather than in science, her main interest. The teacher asked the students to remember a similar conflict they had with a parent or a sibling and write a brief paragraph about how they felt.

This exercise would address which of the following instructional goals?

a. Encourage students to use writing as a means for personal exploration and self-expression.
b. Encourage students to disagree with their parents or siblings on issues that might be important to them.
c. Encourage students to understand the structure of a contemporary novel.
d. Encourage students to understand how a plot is developed through conflict.

29. A third-grade teacher has several students reading above grade level. Most of the remaining students are reading at grade level. There are also a few students reading below grade level. She decides to experiment. Her hypothesis is that by giving the entire class a chapter book above grade level, high-level readers will be satisfied, grade-level readers will be challenged in a positive way, and students reading below grade level will be inspired to improve. Her method is most likely to:

a. Succeed, producing students reading at an Instructional reading level. High-level readers will be happy to be given material appropriate to their reading level. Grade-level readers will challenge themselves to improve reading strategies in order to master the text. Because only a few of the students are reading below grade level, the other students, who feel happy and energized, will inspire the slower readers by modeling success.
b. Succeed, producing students reading at an Independent reading level. High-level readers will independently help grade-level readers who will, in turn, independently help those below grade level.
c. Fail, producing students at a Frustration reading level. Those reading below grade level are likely to give up entirely. Those reading at grade level are likely to get frustrated and form habits that will actually slow down their development.
d. Fail, producing students reading at a Chaotic reading level. By nature, children are highly competitive. The teacher has not taken into consideration multiple learning styles. The children who are at grade level will either become bitter and angry at those whose reading level is above grade level or simply give up. The children reading below grade level will not be able to keep up and will in all likelihood act out their frustration or completely shut down.

30. The English teacher read a statement by Benjamin Franklin and asked her students what made this writing so memorable.

> Early to bed and early to rise, makes a man healthy, wealthy, and wise.
> *Poor Richard's Almanack*, October 1735.

a. use of alliteration
b. use of parallel construction
c. use of metaphors
d. use of similes

Mathematics

31. If an odd number is added to an even number, then which of the following must be true of the result?

a. It is odd
b. It is even
c. It is positive
d. It is zero

32. Which of the following is equal to 6.19×10^3?

a. 0.00619
b. 0.0619
c. 619
d. 6,190

33. What is the area of a square with a perimeter of 16 feet?

a. 4 ft^2
b. 16 ft^2
c. 32 ft^2
d. 256 ft^2

34. Which of the following is equal to $4\sqrt{2^4}$?

a. 4
b. 8
c. 16
d. 32

35. A class contains an equal number of boys and girls. The average height of the boys is 62 inches. The average height of the all the students is 60 inches. What is the average height of the girls in the class?

a. 57 inches
b. 58 inches
c. 59 inches
d. 60 inches

36. A circle has an area equal to 36π. What is its diameter?

a. 4
b. 6
c. 12
d. 4π

37. A dartboard is divided into 8 black and 8 white wedge-shaped sectors so that when a dart is thrown it has a 50% chance of landing on white and a 50% chance of landing on black. If a dart is thrown 3 times in a row and lands on black each time, what is the chance that it will land again on black if it is thrown a fourth time?

a. 12.5%
b. 25%
c. 50%
d. 100%

38. How many integers exist between the numbers –4.2 and 6.1?

a. 2
b. 6
c. 10
d. 11

39. Which of the following expressions represents "five times a number m squared"?

a. $\frac{5}{m^2}$
b. $5m^2$
c. $(5m)^2$
d. $5 + m^2$

40. The radius of a circle with an area of 31 square units is doubled. What is the area of the new circle?

a. 62 square units
b. 93 square units
c. 124 square units
d. 132 square units

41. If $3x + 5 = 11$, then what is the value of x?

a. 6
b. 3
c. 2
d. 1

42. Rachel spent \$24.15 on produce. She bought 2 pounds of onions, 3 pounds of carrots, and $1\frac{1}{2}$ pounds of mushrooms. If the onions cost \$3.69 per pound and the carrots cost \$4.29 per pound, what is the price per pound of mushrooms?

a. \$2.25
b. \$2.60
c. \$2.80
d. \$3.10

43. Which of the following is the solution to the inequality $4x - 12 < 4$?

a. $x < 2$
b. $x > 2$
c. $x > 4$
d. $x < 4$

44. If $a = -6$ and $b = 7$, then $4a(3b + 5) + 2b =$?

a. 638
b. -485
c. 850
d. -610

45. Mark is leaving a job site and moving equipment to Phoenix which is located 210 miles north. He drives the first ten miles in 12 minutes. If he continues at the same rate, what will the total travel time be?

a. 3 hours 15 minutes
b. 3 hours 45 minutes
c. 4 hours 12 minutes
d. 4 hours 20 minutes

46. An airplane leaves Atlanta at 2 PM and flies north at 250 miles per hour. A second airplane leaves Atlanta 30 minutes later and flies north at 280 miles per hour. At what time will the second airplane overtake the first?

a. 6:00 PM
b. 6:20 PM
c. 6:40 PM
d. 7:00 PM

47. The table below shows the cost of renting a bicycle for 1, 2, or 3 hours. Which answer choice shows the equation that best represents the data? Let *C* represent the cost of the rental and *h* stand for the number of hours of rental time.

Hours	1	2	3
Cost	\$3.60	\$7.20	\$10.80

a. $C = 3.60h$
b. $C = h + 3.60$
c. $C = 3.60h + 10.80$
d. $C = \frac{10.80}{h}$

48. Chan receives a bonus from his job. He pays 30% in taxes, gives 30% to charity, and uses another 25% to pay off an old debt. He has \$600 left. What was the total amount of Chan's bonus?

a. \$4,000
b. \$3,600
c. \$3,200
d. \$3,000

49. A student is presented with the following problem: $4^2 + 5(4 \times 3) - 10$. Which operation should the student perform first?

a. Multiplying five by four and three
b. Squaring four
c. Subtracting ten from three
d. Adding four and five

50. A student is asked to find the perimeter of a shape with four sides of different length. Which general equation suggests the calculation the student will need to perform?

a. $P = 4^2$
b. $P = x^4$
c. $P = a + b + c + d$
d. $P = 2x + 2y$

51. Students are working on telling time. The teacher adjusts the hands of a clock and asks the students to say what time it is. One student says "ten two." To what time is the student probably referring?

a. 2:02
b. 2:10
c. 10:10
d. 10:02

52. Students are given the following word problem: "A man needs to make fifty cupcakes. Each of his baking trays will hold eight cupcakes. How many baking trays will the man need?" One student determines the answer to be 6.25. Why is this answer incorrect?

a. The answer should be expressed as a mixed number.
b. Baking trays cannot be subdivided.
c. The student's arithmetic is incorrect.
d. The student should round down to six.

53. A student is asked to find 3/5 of 75. Which of the following expressions could the student use?

a. (3 × 75) ÷ 5
b. 75 ÷ 0.6
c. Either A or B
d. Neither A nor B

54. Students are given the following algebra problem: $2x + 5 = 20$. One student comes up with an answer of $x = 12.5$. Is the student correct? If not, what has the student most likely done wrong?

a. Yes, the student's answer is correct.
b. No, the student has not rounded up to 13.
c. No, the student has probably not divided both sides by 2.
d. No, the student has most likely added 5 to both sides rather than subtracting.

55. 4(3 × 7) ÷ 8 = ?

A student created the above number sentence to solve the following problem: "Divide the sum of the products of four and three and four and seven by eight."

What is the correct number sentence for this problem?

a. (4 + 3)(4 + 7) ÷ 8 = ?
b. (4 × 3)(4 × 7) ÷ 8 = ?
c. 4(3 + 7) ÷ 8 = ?
d. The student's number sentence is correct.

56. Students are asked to add 3/8 and 5/6. What must be their first step?

a. Finding the lowest common denominator
b. Multiplying three by five
c. Finding the greatest common factor
d. Adding three and five

57. A student is asked to find the factors of 32. She comes up with the following list: 1, 2, 4, 8, 16, 32. Is this list correct?

a. Yes, it includes all the factors of 32.
b. Yes, but it omits several additional possible factors.
c. No, it contains several terms that are not factors of 32.
d. No, it is a list of the multiples rather than the factors of 32.

58. Students are presented with the following word problem:

"Five basketball teams participate in a round-robin tournament, where each team plays all of the other teams one time. How many games will be played in the tournament?"

Which equation could students use to solve this problem?

a. $(5 \times 4) \div 2 = ?$
b. $5 + 4 + 3 + 2 + 1 = ?$
c. $4 \times 3 \times 2 \times 1 = ?$
d. $5 \times 5 = ?$

59. Students are asked to list pairs of terms that have a ratio of 5 : 4. Which of these pairs should not be on the list?

a. 25 and 20
b. 15 and 12
c. 35 and 24
d. 55 and 44

60. Students are given the following word problem: "A man begins driving west at an average speed of 45 miles per hour. After two and half hours, how far will he have driven?" Which expression should students devise to answer this question?

a. 45×2.30
b. $45 \div 2.30$
c. $45 \div 2.5$
d. 45×2.5

Writing

Refer to the following for questions 61–65:

The following sentences test correctness and effectiveness of expression. Part of each sentence or the entire sentence is underlined; beneath each sentence are four ways of phrasing the underlined material. Choice A repeats the original phrasing; the other three choices are different. For each question in this section, select the best answer from the choices given.

61. <u>The family, as a whole, are united</u> against the sale of the land.

a. The family, as a whole, are united
b. The family, as a whole, is united
c. As a whole, the family are united
d. The family are united as a whole

62. Anyone on the girls' Junior Varsity Team <u>were invited to put her name</u> on the list to try out for the Varsity Team.

a. were invited to put her name
b. was invited to put her name
c. are invited to put her name
d. put her name by invitation

63. All last summer, despite the sweltering heat and humidity, <u>I wear a suit, tie, and closed shoes for work.</u>

a. I wear a suit, tie, and closed shoes for work.
b. I nevertheless wear a suit, tie, and closed shoes for work.
c. I wear a suit, a tie, and closed shoes for work.
d. I wore a suit, tie, and closed shoes for work.

64. People who like jazz don't usually turn into <u>someone who likes country music</u>.

a. someone who likes country music
b. someone who also likes country music
c. people who like country music
d. people who likes country music

65. We all are unique and <u>each of us has our own way</u> of solving problems.

a. each of us has our own way
b. each of us have our own way
c. has our own way
d. each have our own way

Refer to the following for questions 66–70:

(1) Kids and people need to spend more time outside on a daily basis. (2) <u>Last Child in the Woods: Saving Our Children from Nature-Deficit Disorder</u> is by Richard Louv and who says that in the last 30 years kids have become increasingly removed from nature to their detriment. (3) A 1991 study found that the radius children are allowed to roam outside their homes has shrunk to 1/9 of what it was 20 years before.

(4) Very bad for their physical fitness and mental health. (5) One in 5 American children is obese—compared with one in 20 in the late 1960s—and nearly 8 million kids suffer from mental illnesses, including depression and attention deficit disorder. (6) He says playing in nature helps reduce stress, increase concentration and promote problem-solving, this can help kids with attention deficit disorder and many other problems. (7) Nature play can increase a child's self-confidence and independence.

(8) Parents are scared to let kids play in the woods. (9) Parents are increasingly afraid of child abduction. (10) This is a terrible thing but actually very rare and fear of them should be balanced against the effect of fear on our daily lives.

(11) Kids play too many video games, watch too much television and are in the car for long stretches of time. (12) It is important to have the experience of wet feet and dirty hands and not just read about a frog, for example but to hold it in your hands.

(13) Parents and emphasize organized sports over imaginative play. (14) It's great that kids play so much organized sports now, but activity and physical play used to be what kids did with their free time, not twice a week for soccer practice.

66. Consider the following excerpt from the passage.

Sentence 2: *Last Child in the Woods: Saving Our Children from Nature-Deficit Disorder* is by Richard Louv and who says that in the last 30 years kids have become increasingly removed from nature to their detriment.

Select the best version of the underlined portion.

a. is by Richard Louv and who says that in the last 30 years kids have become increasingly removed
b. is by Richard Louv, who says that in the last 30 years kids have become increasingly removed
c. is by Richard Louv and he says that in the last 30 years kids have become increasingly removed
d. is by Richard Louv he says that in the last 30 years kids have become increasingly removed

67. Which of the following is the most succinct and clear way to rewrite sentences 8 and 9?

a. Parents are scared to let kids play in the woods and are increasingly afraid of child abduction.
b. Parents are scared to let kids play in the woods because they are increasingly afraid of child abduction.
c. Parents are scared to let kids play in the woods so they are increasingly afraid of child abduction.
d. Parents are scared to let kids play in the woods or be abducted.

68. Which of the following represents the best version of sentence 4?

a. It is very bad for their physical fitness and mental health.
b. This is very bad for their physical fitness and mental health.
c. Which is very bad for their physical fitness and mental health.
d. This "nature-deficit disorder" is very bad for their physical fitness and mental health.

69. Sentence 10 is poorly written. What can we infer the initial *This* of the sentence refers to?

a. Parents
b. Kids
c. Woods
d. Child abduction

70. The paragraph that includes sentences 11 and 12 does NOT contain a clear point. Which of the following best describes what the author is likely trying to communicate in this paragraph?

a. Nature is important.
b. It is a problem that kids are increasingly entertained by technology rather than by the sensory experience of nature.
c. It is a problem that kids are removed from nature.
d. Kids should get their hands and feet dirty in some way very often.

Refer to the following for questions 71–72:

My Trip to the Fire Station

By Derek

(1) Last week me and my class went to the fire station to look at the engines. (2) We was in the bus and going to the station when Ms. Glass said everybody needed to look out the window. (3) We heard the sirens and then as we got to the station a truck drove past with its lights going. (4) It was only one of the trucks at the station so we still got to do the tour just like we were supposed to. (5) One of the firemen let us try on his coat and it was real heavy. (6) It was a great trip for the class. (7) We also met the dog that lives at the station and we slid down the pole one at a time.

71. Which correction should be made to sentence (1)?

a. Eliminate the words *me and.*
b. Substitute *I* for *me.*
c. Eliminate the words *to look at the engines.*
d. Place a comma after *week.*

72. Which sentence should be moved to a different place in the essay?

a. Sentence (1)
b. Sentence (3)
c. Sentence (4)
d. Sentence (6)

73. A student is composing a short persuasive essay about the importance of recycling. Which of the following would be the most effective thesis statement?

a. "Recycling reduces waste and the consumption of natural resources."
b. "People who don't recycle hate this planet."
c. "Recycling is a fun way to make a difference."
d. "I have recycled for my entire life."

74. A student writes the following sentence in a short story:

"We'll see what the commitee says," Darrell said to his sisters' friend.

The student has made an error of

a. punctuation.
b. grammar.
c. spelling.
d. diction.

75. Which of the following would be the best reference material for a fourth-grader's paper about space shuttles?

a. scientific journal
b. dictionary
c. encyclopedia
d. newspaper

76. A student's essay contains the following run-on sentence:

After playing baseball we went to the pool and we swam the water was cool.

Which of the following corrections is best?

a. We played baseball, went to the pool, and swam, and the water was cool.
b. After playing baseball, we went to the pool and swam in the cool water.
c. We played baseball and swam in the pool's cool water.
d. We played baseball, and then we went to the pool. We swam in the cool water.

77. A student's essay contains the following sentence:

After I watched the movie that afternoon, I spent the next week thinking about how to build a rocket.

What must the student do to correct this sentence?

a. The initial clause should be written, "After I had watched the movie that afternoon."
b. The comma should be eliminated.
c. The phrase "the next week" should be moved to the end of the sentence.
d. Nothing, the sentence is correct as written.

78. A student's essay contains the following sentence:

He claimed that he never went into the clubhouse with red paint.

The student has made an error of

a. punctuation.
b. spelling.
c. grammar.
d. diction.

79. Which word is NOT spelled correctly?

a. nuisance
b. prairie
c. mysterious
d. Wendesday

80. A student's essay contains the following sentence:

David Jackson, Jr., complained that the car had lost it's air-conditioning.

What must the student do to correct this sentence?

a. Substitute *lossed* for *lost.*
b. Eliminate the period after *Jr.*
c. Eliminate the comma after *Jr.*
d. Substitute *its* for *it's*

Refer to the following for questions 81–86:

(1) One of the pioneer sculptors of the nineteenth century was Honore Daumier (1810-1879). (2) He is well-known particularly for caricature heads that were created between 1830 and 1832. (3) His later works anticipate the work of Rodin, what with their highly cut-out surfaces offset by studied, flowing poses.

(4) Although Daumier was one of the first modern sculptors, his work did not serve as an influence to later artists. (5) This is because nearly all of the other artists of the time hardly ever got to see any of it. (6) This is also true of the sculpture of Degas, who was known as a painter rather than a sculptor, and whose sculpture also was not widely exhibited at the time. (7) And yet, Degas was clearly the greatest sculptor of the era. (8) His bronze casts of dancers and horses retain the layered feeling of the wax models that were their first versions. (9) His more complex scenes seem like crosses between sculpture and painting. (10) When looked at more closely, they display a feeling of mass that the painted canvas cannot by itself convey. (11) It is the interplay between the separate masses in these scenes that involves the viewer and gives them their sense of intrigue.

81. Consider the following excerpt from the passage.

Sentence 2: He is well-known particularly for caricature heads that were created between 1830 and 1832.

Select the best version of the underlined portion.

a. NO CHANGE
b. He is well known, particularly
c. He is particularly well known
d. He is well known particularly

82. Consider the following excerpt from the passage.

Sentence 3: His later works anticipate the work of Rodin, what with their highly cut-out surfaces offset by studied, flowing poses.

Select the best version of the underlined portion.

a. NO CHANGE
b. of Rodin; what with highly cut out surfaces
c. of Rodin, with highly cut-out surfaces
d. of Rodin, with cut-out surfaces

83. Which is the best version of sentence 5?

a. NO CHANGE
b. This is because it was almost never exhibited at the time.
c. His work was hardly ever exhibited.
d. This is because they hardly ever saw any of it.

84. What correction should be made to sentence 6?

a. Add "In addition," to the beginning of the sentence.
b. Delete the clause "and whose sculpture was also not widely exhibited at the time."
c. Change the words "sculpture of Degas" to read "work of Degas".
d. Change "This is also true" to "This was also true".

85. Which sentence is best inserted after sentence 7?

a. A large body of his sculpted works can be found in museums today.
b. His paintings were famous even before the time of his death.
c. He made sculptures out of bronze, stone, and even wood.
d. You can see pictures of his work in many books.

86. Which is best added to the beginning of sentence 10?

a. Increasingly,
b. And yet,
c. Beneath this,
d. However,

Refer to the following for questions 87–88:

Setting Up a Tent

By Darnell

(1) I been campin a bunch of tims with my dad. (2) Wen you go campin you caint sit on the grond so yo gots to get a tent to slep in. (3) The best wons are mad of shiny materrl so the water caint get in. (4) First you gots to fine a flat plac to put yur tent in then you spreds it ot on the grend. (5) Yu puts in the pols and then it props up an you puts in the staks. (6) Wen you is don you can unzip it an get in an slep. (7) You better hav a sleping bag ur som blankets to slep in.

87. This essay suggests that the student needs remedial help with

a. vocabulary.
b. phonics.
c. spelling.
d. reading comprehension.

88. Which sentence would be the best thesis statement for this essay?

a. Sentence (1)
b. Sentence (2)
c. Sentence (4)
d. Sentence (7)

89. Which of the following sentences demonstrates subject-verb agreement?

a. "The beautiful shores of Hawaii is where I call home."
b. "Neither Harriet nor her sister are going to visit him."
c. "The people of the Iroquois Nation are in agreement."
d. "Only one of these islands have a civilized population."

90. Of the following writing examples, which one reflects an error in grammar?

a. "She is without a doubt the very best freind I have ever had in my life."
b. "He said we should wait two hours, we waited two hours and returned."
c. "A great animal lover, his pets included dogs, cats, horses, and chickens."
d. "They were traveling South at first, but later in the trip they went West."

Answer Key and Explanations for Test #1

Reading

1. B: The Russian population of Latvia decreased the most since 1991. The Latvian population decreased slightly, but not to the same degree. The Ukrainian population decreased by an even smaller percentage since 1991. The German population remained relatively unchanged between 1991 and 2011.

2. C: On the chart, the only ethnic group that represents approximately one percent of the population after World War II and approximately three percent by 1991 is the Ukrainian population. The Latvian and Russian populations represent much larger percentages of the total population of Latvia. The German population decreased significantly during this time period.

3. D: The passage states that World War II ended in 1945. The chart shows that the German population began falling in 1935, so there is a slight decrease from 1945 to 1959. While the Ukrainian population's net change was small, it did rise and fall more than the German population's net change. The Latvian and Russian populations fluctuated much more than the German population did over the entire period reflected on the chart, including after 1945.

4. C: The tricky thing about this question is that all the choices are true statements about things said in the essay. Only one, however, is the main idea. The best way to find it is to go to the first paragraph. In it, the author calls the ability to tell true and false statements apart "one of the main goals of every police officer." He goes further, calling this ability "the only way to punish the guilty, exonerate the innocent, and do the most possible good in preventing future crimes." Choice C, therefore, is the correct answer.

5. A: If there is one point that the author has repeated many times in this article, it is that police need to be able to investigate lies to conduct investigations. Therefore, choice A is the correct answer.

6. C: In paragraph 2, the author states that "smoke" lies "slow down an investigation." Therefore, Choice C is the correct response.

7. C: Point of view refers to the vantage point from which a story is written. First person uses the pronoun *I*. Second person uses the pronoun *you*. Third person uses the pronouns *he/she/they*. There is no fourth-person point of view. This passage was written in the third person.

8. B: The words *mysterious* and *important* used in the sentence help the reader deduce that Jo looked secretive. Jo did not look jubilant (joyful), disheveled (disarrayed), or angry.

9. C: The last sentence states that Laurie was "an incorrigible tease." From this statement you can infer that Laurie was unruly or unmanageable. *Stoic* means not showing passion or emotion. *Taciturn* means silent. *Uncanny* means supernatural. There is nothing in the passage to imply he had any of these characteristics.

10. B: Both of the speakers are arguing over how uniforms will affect students, though they are going about it in different ways. Choices A and D are details mentioned in Vivian Harris's argument, but they contradict the points made in Lisa Grant's argument. Choice C could align with Lisa Grant's argument, but neither student's argument suggests that students should focus more on school.

11. C: This detail would only really support the argument against wearing school uniforms, as it introduces evidence that shows that uniforms are not always a preferable option. The other three choices could all appear as details in support of either side of the argument since each detail is objective and neutral.

12. C: Choice C is a primary source that would contain information relevant to Vivian's argument. Choice A is a primary source, but it includes information that is contrary to Vivian's argument. Choice B supports Vivian's position, but articles are secondary sources, so it is incorrect. Choice D could be a secondary or tertiary source, but it is not a primary source. It would also be ineffective for Vivian to use a source she wrote herself to support her own argument, so choice D is incorrect.

13. C: The passage states that a pluralistic society means one that embraces "many points of view," which is closest in meaning to choice C, *tolerant*.

14. B: This passage does not choose one point of view on the issue, so only choice B is in keeping with the passage's purpose, which is to explain the disagreements between the earliest political parties in the US.

15. B: The word *competitive* means that the country would be able to compete financially with other countries. Choice B, stronger, is the best choice.

16. A: *It* refers to the noun *identity*. Choice A is the best choice.

17. B: Since the passage does not choose to argue a particular point of view, the best choice would be the most neutral statement, choice B.

18. D: The stronger the central government, the stronger the country best reflects the true position of the Federalist Party.

19. A: The federal government should not have too much power best represents the Democratic-Republican Party's perspective.

20. B: The final paragraph mentions the Civil War only to show that these differing perspectives would not be easily reconciled. Choice B is the best answer.

21. B: The passage explains the conflicting interests the Democratic-Republican Party and the Federalist Party represent. Choice B best reflects that point.

22. B: Students could recognize the signal words. A is incorrect because defining historical events would not help recognition of comparison and contrast or cause and effect. C is incorrect since a timeline would not help recognition of comparison and contrast or cause and effect. D is incorrect since maps would not help recognition of comparison and contrast or cause and effect.

23. C: The titles are in chronological order. A is incorrect because the titles do not show comparison and contrast. B is incorrect because the titles do not show cause and effect. D is incorrect because the titles do not show problem and solution.

24. D: Hidden message techniques have increased through the years. A is incorrect because hidden message techniques have not remained the same through the years. B is incorrect because hidden message techniques have not decreased through the years. C is incorrect because hidden message techniques have not decreased in importance.

25. C: The teacher is involving them in the concept of faith through Bonhoeffer's life. A is incorrect because details of World War II are not discussed.

B is incorrect because details of Germany are not discussed. D is incorrect because the teacher is not primarily providing a multicultural true story.

26. A: The passage is colloquial. B is incorrect because the passage is not abstract. C is incorrect because the passage is not formal. D is incorrect because the passage is not allusive.

27. B: The author indicated that she revised her books. A is incorrect because the author indicated that revisions were always necessary in her books. C is incorrect because the author did not suggest that revisions showed an inability to write a piece initially. D is incorrect because the author would not have revised her work if it had not improved it.

28. A: This brief paragraph will encourage students to use writing as a means for personal exploration and self-expression. B is incorrect because this writing assignment is not a mandate to disagree with others. C is incorrect because the structure of the novel is not shown in the passage. D is incorrect because the plot of the novel is not shown in the passage.

29. C: This method is likely to fail, producing students at a Frustration reading level. Those reading below grade level are likely to give up entirely. Those reading at grade level are likely to get frustrated and form habits that will actually slow down their development. Giving students texts that are too far beyond their reach produces frustrated readers. In an effort to succeed, frustrated readers are likely to apply strategies that have worked for them in the past but cannot work in this case because the text is simply beyond them. Looking for contextual clues to understand the meaning of unfamiliar words requires that most of the words in the passage are familiar. Breaking unfamiliar words into individual phonemes or syllables can be effective, but not if the number of such words is excessive. In this case, students below reading level and students at reading level will become frustrated when the skills that have worked for them in the past now fail.

30. B: This is use of parallel construction. A is incorrect because this is not use of alliteration. C is incorrect because this is not use of metaphors. D is incorrect because this is not use of similes.

Mathematics

31. A: An odd number can be considered as an even number N plus 1. Two even numbers added together produce an even number, so the result of adding an odd and an even number must be an even number plus 1, which is odd. For example, $4 + 3 = 7$, and 7 is odd.

32. D: In scientific notation, the exponent indicates the number of places that the decimal must be moved to the right. For example, $2.3 \times 10^1 = 2.3 \times 10 = 23$. Moving the decimal three places to the right in this problem is equivalent to multiplying by 1,000, so the result is 6,190.

33. B: The perimeter of a square is 4 times the length of a side. Therefore, in this case, the side must equal $s = 16 \div 4 = 4$. The area is found by squaring the side length, or $A = s^2 = 4^2 = 16$. Therefore, the area is 16 ft^2.

34. C: The square root of a number which is raised to the 4th power is the same number raised to the 2nd power. That is, $\sqrt{2^4} = 2^2 = 4$. Since $4 \times 4 = 16$, choice C is correct.

35. B: The average, or arithmetic mean, is computed by totaling all the measurements and dividing by the number of measurements. Let T_B represent the sum of the heights of the boys in the class, and T_G the sum of the heights of the girls. If N is the number of students in the class, there are $N/2$ boys and $N/2$ girls. The average height of the boys is then $\frac{T_B}{\frac{N}{2}} = \frac{2T_B}{N} = 62$. Similarly, the average height of the girls is $\frac{2T_G}{N}$. The average height of all the students is equal to $\frac{T_B+T_G}{N} = \frac{T_B}{N} + \frac{T_G}{N} = 60$. Therefore, $\frac{T_G}{N} = 60 - \frac{T_B}{N} = 60 - 31 = 29$, and the average height for the girls is $2 \times 29 = 58$.

36. C: The area of a circle is equal to πr^2, where r is the radius. Therefore, $\pi r^2 = 36\pi$, and $r = \sqrt{36} = 6$. Since the diameter is twice the radius, it is equal to 12.

37. C: Each throw of the dart is an independent event and has no influence on the outcome of any other throw. Every time the dart is thrown, it has a 50% chance of landing on black, irrespective of the results of previous throws.

38. D: The integers between –4.2 and 6.1 are –4, –3, –2, –1, 0, 1, 2, 3, 4, 5, and 6. Therefore, there are 11 integers between –4.2 and 6.1.

39. B: The verbal description "five times a number m squared" means that m must be squared, and the resulting number multiplied by 5. This is represented by the expression $5m^2$. Choice C is incorrect because the value within the parentheses is evaluated first, so that both 5 and m are squared. This results in a value of $25m^2$, which is incorrect.

40. C: The area scales with the square of the radius, so if the radius increases in length by a factor of 2, the area will increase by 2^2, or 4. Since Area $= \pi r^2$, if the radius r is replaced with $2r$, this yields Area $= \pi(2r)^2 = 4\pi r^2$, which is 4 times the original area.

$$31 \times 4 = 124$$

Therefore, the area of the new circle is 124 square units.

41. C: Solve the equation using inverse operations. First, subtract 5 from both sides.

$$3x + 5 = 11$$
$$3x + 5 - 5 = 11 - 5$$
$$3x = 6$$

Then, divide both sides by 3.

$$\frac{3x}{3} = \frac{6}{3}$$
$$x = 2$$

Therefore, the value of x is 2.

42. B: To answer this question, we first determine the total cost of the onions and carrots, since these prices are given. This will equal $2 \times \$3.69 + 3 \times \$4.29 = \$20.25$. Next, this sum is subtracted from the total cost of the produce to determine the cost of the mushrooms: $\$24.15 - \$20.25 = \$3.90$. Finally, the cost of the mushrooms is divided by the quantity in pounds to determine the cost per pound:

$$\text{Cost per lb} = \frac{\$3.90}{1.5} = \$2.60$$

Therefore, the mushrooms cost \$2.60 per pound.

43. D: Use inverse operations to solve the inequality. Begin by adding 12 to both sides.

$$4x - 12 < 4$$
$$4x - 12 + 12 < 4 + 12$$
$$4x < 16$$

Then, divide both sides by 4.

$$\frac{4x}{4} < \frac{16}{4}$$
$$x < 4$$

Therefore, the solution to the inequality is $x < 4$.

44. D: First, compute the value enclosed by the parentheses, $3b + 5 = 3 \times 7 + 5 = 26$. Next, compute $4a = -24$. Note that a is negative, so that this product is negative as well. The product $4a(3b + 5)$ will therefore be negative as well and equals -624. Finally, add the value of $2b$, or $2 \times 7 = 14$, to -624, to get the final answer $-624 + 14 = -610$.

45. C: Since the rate, in miles per minute, is constant, this can be solved by setting up a proportion.

$$\frac{\text{miles}}{\text{min}} = \frac{10}{12} = \frac{210}{t}$$

Now, solve for t by using cross multiplication.

$$t = \frac{210 \times 12}{10} = 252$$

Mark will take 252 minutes to reach his destination. From here, convert the time to hours and minutes. Start by dividing 252 by 60.

$$252 \div 60 = 4.2$$

He will take 4 hours and 0.2 of another hour. To convert the partial hour, 0.2, to minutes, multiply it by 60.

$$0.2 \times 60 = 12$$

Therefore, it will take him 4 hours and 12 minutes to reach his destination.

46. C: Define the variable t as the elapsed time (in hours) from the time the first airplane takes off. Then, at any time, the distance traveled by the first plane is $d_1 = 250t$. The second plane takes off 30 minutes later so that at any time, the distance that it has traveled is $d_2 = 280(t - 0.5)$. This plane will overtake the first when the two distances are equal, which is when $d_1 = d_2$, or when $250t = 280(t - 0.5)$. First, use the distributive property to get rid of the parentheses.

$$250t = 280t - 140$$

Next, subtract $280t$ from each side of the equation.

$$-30t = -140$$

Next, divide both sides by −30.

$$t \approx 4.67$$

This yields an elapsed time of 4.667 hours, or 4 hours and 40 minutes. Since the first plane left at 2 PM, 4 hours and 40 minutes later is 6:40 PM.

47. A: This equation is a linear relationship that has a slope of 3.60 and passes through the origin. The table shows that for each hour of rental, the cost increases by $3.60. This matches with the slope of the equation. Of course, if the bicycle is not rented at all (0 hours), there will be no charge ($0). If plotted on the Cartesian plane, the line would have a y-intercept of 0. The first choice is the only one that meets these requirements.

48. A: Besides the $600 he has remaining, Chan has paid out a total of 85% (30% + 30% + 25%) of his bonus for the expenses described in the question. Therefore, the $600 represents the remaining 15%. Remember that 15% can be written as $\frac{15}{100}$. To determine his total bonus, solve $\frac{15}{100}x = 600$. So, $x = \frac{100}{15} \times 600 = 4{,}000$, and Chan's total bonus is $4,000.

49. A: The first operation to be performed is multiplying five by four and three. This question requires knowledge of the order of operations, or the sequence in which arithmetic functions should be performed in a complex number sentence. The order of operations is parentheses, exponents, multiplication, addition, and subtraction. In this problem, the first step is to resolve the parenthetical expression. This can be done either by multiplying five by four and three and then multiplying the products, or by multiplying four and three and then multiplying this product by five.

50. C: The equation $P = a + b + c + d$ suggests the necessary calculation for this problem. Perimeter is found by adding the lengths of the sides together. Since the four sides of this shape are known to have varying lengths, they must be represented by four different variables. If the shape was a rectangle (that is, if it had two sets of two equal sides), choice D could be correct.

51. C: When a student gives the answer "ten two," he is probably referring to 10:10. Students who are learning to read an analog clock will often confuse hours with minutes. A student who gives the minutes as "two" most likely sees the minute hand over the two, which actually indicates ten minutes past the hour.

52. B: The student's answer is incorrect because baking trays cannot be subdivided. In other words, a baking tray only comes in units of one, so the man in the word problem will need seven trays. The last tray will be filled only one quarter of the way full. This problem underscores the necessity of reading comprehension when solving word problems. Students should not just translate the terms of the word problem into the language of math. They must also check to make sure their method and solution is logical.

53. A: The student could use (3 × 75) ÷ 5 to solve this problem. Answer choice A could be expressed 3/5 × 75/1, which simplifies to (3 × 75)/5 = 225/5 = 45. The answer then is that 3/5 of 75 is 45.

54. D: The student's answer is incorrect, most likely because the student has added rather than subtracted 5 to both sides. When solving a simple algebraic equation of this type, the goal is to isolate the variable on one side. This is done by eliminating the other terms and coefficients one by one. The most common first step in this problem would be to eliminate the 5 by subtracting an equal amount from both sides of the equation. This would leave $2x = 15$, which leads to the correct solution $x = 7.5$. If 5 was added, however, the resulting equation would be $2x = 25$, which would lead to the student's incorrect answer.

55. C: The number sentence should be written 4(3 + 7) ÷ 8. The student erred by placing a multiplication symbol in between the three and seven. The problem states that the sum of the products of four and three and four and seven is to be divided by eight. In other words, four must be multiplied by both three and seven, with the resulting products added together. One way to express this is 4(3 + 7). Another would be 4 × 3 + 4 × 7.

56. A: The first step in this operation must be finding the lowest common denominator. Fractions may not be added together or subtracted from one another unless they have the same denominator. The lowest common denominator is found by listing the multiples of the denominators until a common multiple is found. In this case, the lists would proceed as 8, 16, 24 and 6, 12, 18, 24, indicating that the lowest common denominator is 24. To convert 3/8 into a fraction with a denominator of 24, numerator and denominator must be multiplied by 3: 3/8 × 3/3 = 9/24. To convert 5/6 into a fraction with a denominator of 24, both numerator and denominator must be multiplied by 4: 5/6 × 4/4 = 20/24. With common denominators, then, the problem can now be solved: 9/24 + 20/24 = 29/24, or 1 5/24.

57. A: The student's list is correct and comprehensive: it contains all of the factors of 32. The factors of a number are all of those whole numbers that can be divided evenly into the given number. Another way of expressing this is that the factors of a number are all of the terms that can be used in a two-term multiplication problem that produces the given number. The following multiplication problems produce 32: 32 × 1, 16 × 2, and 8 × 4. These are the factors of 32.

58. A: Students could use the equation $(5 \times 4) \div 2 = ?$ to solve this problem. There are five teams, each of which will play for others. This accounts for the 5 × 4. However, each game includes two teams, so the product must be divided by two. Otherwise, the student would be counting Team A's game against Team B as well as Team B's game against Team A.

59. C: 35 and 24 should not be on this list because they do not have a ratio of $5 : 4$. The ratio of 35 to 24 cannot be simplified. Pairs of numbers will only have the correct ratio if they can be produced by multiplying 5 and 4 by the same numbers. For instance, 25 and 20 are produced by multiplying 5 and 4 by 5. 15 and 12 are produced by multiplying 5 and 4 by 3. 55 and 44 are produced by multiplying 5 and 4 by 11.

60. D: Students should use the expression 45×2.5 to answer this question.

Writing

61. B: The word "family" is singular. The verb thus needs to be the singular "is," rather than the plural "are."

62. B: The word "anyone" is singular, so the phrasing "were invited" is incorrect.

63. D: "All last summer" indicates a time in the past, so the present tense form of "to wear" is incorrect.

64. C: The word "people" is plural and is incorrectly matched with the singular word "someone."

65. A: Sentence is correct.

66. B: The part of the sentence "who says that…" is a parenthetical phrase about Richard Louv, not about the subject of the sentence. The *and who* is therefore incorrect, and the phrase needs to be set off from the sentence by a comma.

67. B: The best answer is (B) because it best captures the logical connection of the sentences: the fear of abduction is the reason that parents are afraid to let kids play in the woods.

68. D: The sentence needs a subject. Answer (D) is the one that most clearly identifies a subject.

69. D: The word *this* most logically refers to child abduction. Although not stated explicitly, it is the only choice that could logically be described as "a terrible thing" and "very rare."

70. B: Although the paragraph does not make its point explicitly, it clearly states that kids are spending too much time with video games and TV (being entertained by technology) and would be helped by more time getting their feet and hands dirty and touching things rather than just reading about them (having a positive sensory experience of nature).

71. A: The student should correct the first sentence by eliminating the words *me and*. Since the student has said that his class went to the fire station, it may be assumed that he went as well. Substituting *I* for *me* would be more grammatically correct, but no less redundant. The other answer choices describe unnecessary changes.

72. D: The sentence "It was a great trip for the class" should be moved to a different place in the essay. This sentence would be an appropriate final statement for the essay. Up until this point, the student has proceeded in chronological order through the events of the day. Sentence (6) breaks this trend to make a more general statement about the field trip. This statement would be more appropriate at the end of the essay.

73. A: The most effective thesis statement would be "Recycling reduces waste and the consumption of natural resources." A thesis statement expresses the main idea of the essay. Any of the answer choices could serve as a thesis statement, depending on the rest of the essay. However, since the question specifies that the assignment is a short persuasive essay, the effectiveness of the other answer choices becomes dubious. Answer choice B is a personal attack, hardly the most effective strategy for persuasion. Answer choice C focuses on the pleasure of recycling, which is not as relevant to its importance as the facts in answer choice A. Answer choice D is an autobiographical statement that has no real bearing on the importance of recycling, and would not be persuasive to a reader.

74. C: The student has made an error of spelling. The correct spelling is *committee*. This sentence contains other details that look questionable but that cannot be called errors out of context. The comma should be placed inside the final quotation mark, and the apostrophe is in the correct place assuming that the author is referring to the friend of more than one of Darrell's sisters.

75. C: An encyclopedia would be the best reference material for a fourth-grader's paper about space shuttles. When answering a question of this type, it is important to note the grade of the student. A fourth-grader is not likely to understand the content of a scientific journal, even though this source may provide the most detailed information about space shuttles. A dictionary merely provides definitions and etymologies, and would not contain sufficient information for an entire paper. A newspaper might reference space shuttles as they figure in current events, but it would not have basic background information on this type of subject.

76. B: The best correction of the student's run-on sentence is "After playing baseball, we went to the pool and swam in the cool water." The other answer choices are grammatically correct, but each of them is weak in another way. Answer choice A has a boring structure, and it is jarring to the reader to introduce a new subject (the water) in the last clause. Answer choice C doesn't clearly indicate the sequence of events, and contains an awkward phrase (*pool's cool*). Answer choice D is choppy and divides the subject matter in an odd way. It makes more sense to group in one sentence the ideas related to swimming.

77. A: To correct this sentence, the student must write the initial clause as "After I had watched the movie that afternoon." This sentence describes two actions that took place in the past. To establish the sequence in which they happened, the student must put the dependent clause in the past perfect tense (had watched) and the independent clause in the past tense. This shows that the student watched the movie before thinking about how to build a rocket.

78. C: The student has made an error of grammar. The placement of the modifying phrase "with red paint" makes it impossible to tell whether the person or the clubhouse had the red paint. If the person had the paint, the sentence could be written as follows: He claimed that he never went with red paint into the clubhouse. If the paint is on the clubhouse, the sentence could be written like this: He claimed that he never went into the clubhouse, which was painted red.

79. D: *Wendesday* is not spelled correctly. The correct spelling is *Wednesday*. This word has an unusual spelling, as the *d* does not sound as if it should come before the *n*. A paraprofessional needs to develop an ability to judge spelling at a glance, so that corrections can be made while students are still working on a draft.

80. D: To correct this sentence, the student must substitute *its* for *it's*. The student has used the contraction for *it is* rather than the possessive form of *it*. The student's handling of *Jr.* is correct. When this title is abbreviated, it should be followed by a period even in the middle of a sentence. Also, it is acceptable to set aside this abbreviation with commas, though this is not mandatory.

81. C: The adverb *particularly* clearly modifies the adjectival phrase *well known*, and no hyphen is needed. Choice B subtly changes the meaning. Choice D corrects the spelling of the original but is a more awkward phrasing.

82. C: Choice C eliminates the slang expression *what with*. Choice D subtly changes the meaning.

83. B: Choice A reads poorly and fails to fully connect why the artists did not see his work. Choice C fails to make the connection with the preceding sentence, establishing itself as the explanation for

Daumier's lack of influence, and choice D fails to explain why other artists did not see Daumier's work.

84. B: Since the sentence begins with "This is also true," the clause in choice B is redundant with the preceding sentence. None of the other choices address this.

85. A: Choice A expands upon the previous sentence by explaining why he is considered the greatest sculptor of the era.

86. D: The word *however* shows that the sentence will provide a contrast to the preceding sentence. Choice B does this as well, but it repeats the same expression used three sentences before.

87. C: This essay suggests that the student needs remedial help with spelling. The essay makes sense, and the student demonstrates sufficient vocabulary to make his point. However, the spelling in this essay is poor. Nevertheless, the spelling errors do not betray a lack of phonics knowledge; indeed, the student's misspellings seem to be the product of simply sounding words out rather than having a solid grasp of English spelling.

88. B: The second sentence of this essay would be the best thesis statement. The title of the essay is "Setting Up a Tent," and the second sentence provides the most general statement of this theme. Of course, none of the sentences in this essay really serves as an effective thesis. The first sentence somewhat introduces the subject of camping but is basically irrelevant to the rest of the essay.

89. C: The verb in option A should be plural "are" to agree with subject "shores," not singular to agree with modifier "Hawaii." Because both subjects "Harriet" and "sister" in option B are singular and so is the construction "Neither… nor," the verb should be singular "is," not plural "are." The verb is correctly plural "are" to agree with subject "people" in option C, not with singular noun "Nation" in the modifying prepositional phrase. The verb should be singular "has" in option D to agree with subject "one," not with modifying plural noun "islands."

90. C: This sentence contains the grammatical error of a misplaced modifier. The modifying phrase "a great animal lover" does NOT modify "his pets" but *him* (e.g., "A great animal lover, *he had* pets including…."). Choice A contains a spelling error: *friend* is misspelled. A common student error is to transpose vowel combinations like this. Choice B has a punctuation error: these two independent clauses should be separated by a semicolon, not a comma. (In this example, a colon would also be acceptable, but not a comma, which creates a run-on sentence.) Choice D has a capitalization error: *South* and *West* are only capitalized when used as names, e.g., "the wild West" or "the sunny South," but when used as directions, they are lowercase.

Practice Test #2

Reading

Refer to the following for questions 1–3:

NOTE: The instructor of a history class has just finished grading the essay exams from his students, and the results are not good. The essay exam was worth 70% of the final course score. The highest score in the class was a low B, and more than half of the class of 65 students failed the exam. In view of this, the instructor reconsiders his grading plan for the semester and sends out an email message to all students.

> Dear Students:
>
> The scores for the essay exam have been posted in the online course grade book. By now, many of you have probably seen your grade and are a little concerned, since this accounts for 70% of your final grade. (And if you're not concerned, you should be—at least a bit!) At the beginning of the semester, I informed the class that I have a strict grading policy and that all scores will stand unquestioned. With each class comes a new challenge, however, and as any good instructor will tell you, sometimes the original plan has to change. As a result,
>
> I propose the following options for students to make up their score:
>
> 1. I will present the class with an extra credit project at the next course meeting. The extra credit project will be worth 150% of the point value of the essay exam that has just been completed. While I will not drop the essay exam score, I will give you more than enough of a chance to make up the difference and raise your overall score.
> 2. I will allow each student to develop his or her own extra credit project. This project may reflect the tenor of option number 1 (above) but will allow the student to create a project more in his or her own line of interest. Bear in mind, however, that this is more of a risk. The scoring for option number 2 will be more subjective, depending on whether or not I feel that the project is a successful alternative to the essay exam. If it is, the student will be awarded up to 150% of the point value of the essay exam.
> 3. I will provide the class with the option of developing a group project. Students may form groups of 3 to 4 and put together an extra credit project that reflects a stronger response to the questions in the essay exam. This extra credit project will also be worth 150% of the point value of the essay exam. Note that each student will receive an equal score for the project, so there is a risk in this as well. If you are part of a group in which you do most of the work, each member of the group will receive equal credit for it. The purpose of the group project is to allow students to work together and arrive at a stronger response than if each worked individually.
>
> If you are interested in pursuing extra credit to make up for the essay exam, please choose <u>one</u> of the options above. No other extra credit opportunities will be provided for the course.
>
> Good luck!
>
> Dr. Edwards

1. Which of the following describes this type of writing?

a. Technical
b. Narrative
c. Persuasive
d. Expository

2. Which of the following quotes offers the best summary for the instructor's motive in sending the email to the students?

a. By now, many of you have probably seen your grade and are a little concerned, since this accounts for 70% of your final grade. (And if you're not concerned, you should be—at least a bit!)
b. With each class comes a new challenge, however, and as any good instructor will tell you, sometimes the original plan has to change.
c. The purpose of the group project is to allow students to work together and arrive at a stronger response than if each worked individually.
d. At the beginning of the semester, I informed the class that I have a strict grading policy and that all scores will stand unquestioned.

3. Based on the passage, which of the following is the most logical conclusion?

a. The professor will offer another extra credit project later in the semester.
b. Students who choose two extra-credit options will be given double the extra credit.
c. Students who choose the third option will receive one quarter of the offered extra credit.
d. Students are most likely to earn maximum extra credit by choosing the first option.

Refer to the following for questions 4–11:

VISUAL PERCEPTION

It is tempting to think that your eyes are simply mirrors that reflect whatever is in front of them. Researchers, however, have shown that your brain is constantly working to create the impression of a continuous, uninterrupted world.

For instance, in the last ten minutes, you have blinked your eyes around 200 times. You have probably not been aware of any of these interruptions in your visual world. Something you probably have not seen in a long time without the aid of a mirror is your nose. It is always right there, down in the bottom corner of your vision, but your brain <u>filters</u> it out so that you are not aware of your nose unless you purposefully look at it.

Nor are you aware of the artery that runs right down the middle of your <u>retina</u>. It creates a large blind spot in your visual field, but you never notice the hole it leaves. To see this blind spot, try the following: Cover your left eye with your hand. With your right eye, look at the O on the left. As you move your head closer to the O, the X will disappear as it enters the blind spot caused by your optical nerve.

O **X**

Your brain works hard to make the world look continuous!

4. The word "filters," as used in this passage, most nearly means:

a. Alternates
b. Reverses
c. Ignores
d. Depends

5. The word "retina," as used in this passage, most nearly means:

a. Optical illusion
b. Part of the eye
c. Pattern
d. Blindness

6. Which of the following statements can be inferred from this passage?

a. Not all animals' brains filter out information.
b. Visual perception is not a passive process.
c. Blind spots cause accidents.
d. The eyes never reflect reality.

7. What is the author's purpose for including the two letters in the middle of the passage?

a. To demonstrate the blind spot in the visual field
b. To organize the passage
c. To transition between the last two paragraphs of the passage
d. To prove that the blind spot is not real

8. What is the main purpose of this passage?

a. To persuade the reader to pay close attention to blind spots
b. To explain the way visual perception works
c. To persuade the reader to consult an optometrist if the O and X disappear
d. To prove that vision is a passive process

9. Based on the passage, which of the following statements is true?

a. The brain cannot accurately reflect reality.
b. Glasses correct the blind spot caused by the optical nerve.
c. Vision is the least important sense.
d. The brain fills in gaps in the visual field.

10. The author mentions the nose to illustrate what point?

a. The brain filters out some visual information.
b. Not all senses work the same way.
c. Perception is a passive process.
d. The sense of smell filters out information.

11. Which of the following statements can be inferred from the second paragraph?

a. The brain filters out the sound created by the shape of the ears.
b. The brain does not perceive all activity in the visual field.
c. Closing one eye affects depth perception.
d. The brain evolved as a result of environmental factors.

Refer to the following for questions 12–19:

Easily the most recognizable constellation in the night sky, the Big Dipper has captured the imaginations of people of every culture and every historical period. Not all people have seen the shape of a dipper, though. In fact, the Big Dipper is only part of a larger constellation called Ursa Major. The seven stars that make up the handle and pan of the Big Dipper are just a few of the eighteen stars that make up Ursa Major, a name the Greeks gave the constellation that means "The Great Bear."

Native Americans also saw the constellation as a bear, but they saw the bear in the cup of the dipper. Some Native American groups saw the stars of the handle as three warriors hunting the bear; others saw them as three cubs following their mother. In England the cluster of stars is thought to resemble a plow, but in Scandinavia it is known as a wagon. In ancient Mayan astronomy, it was called a spoon. Arabic astronomers saw the bowl as a coffin and the three stars in the handle as mourners at a funeral. Others have seen it as a bull's thigh, or even a governmental organization.

American slaves sang a song called "Follow the Drinking Gourd." On one level, the song sounded like it was about the cup the slaves used to drink water, but it also worked as a code to teach slaves who wanted their freedom to escape to the north by following the Big Dipper when traveling by night.

The Big Dipper is circumpolar, so it can be seen all night long. This reason may account in part for its easy visibility among the constellations.

12. As used in the passage, the word "circumpolar" most nearly means:

a. Seasonal
b. Stays in the sky all night
c. Stationary
d. Bright

13. Which statement best describes the author's purpose in writing this passage?

a. To present correct and incorrect interpretations of the Big Dipper.
b. To explain the secret codes of American slaves.
c. To persuade the reader to spend more time viewing the night skies.
d. To inform the reader of different interpretations of the Big Dipper.

14. Which statement can be inferred from the third paragraph?

a. Stars can be used to navigate unknown areas.
b. Slavery was an immoral institution.
c. All old spirituals contain secret messages.
d. Slaves adopted the Native American interpretation of the Big Dipper.

15. Which of the following statements is true of the Native American interpretation of the Big Dipper?

a. The handle was interpreted as mourners at a funeral.
b. Their interpretation was inherited from the Mayan civilization.
c. Some groups interpreted the three stars of the handle differently.
d. They also used the stars to navigate their way to freedom from slavery.

16. Which of the following statements seems true based on the passage?

a. No two cultures share the same interpretation of the Big Dipper.
b. Navigating by the stars has largely been replaced by technology.
c. The stars have inspired the imaginations of many cultures.
d. Myths are often based in truth.

17. According to the passage, the word "code" most nearly means:

a. Cipher
b. Interpretation
c. Secret message
d. Slang

18. According to the passage, which one of the following statements is true of the constellations?

a. Seen from another galaxy, constellations would not appear the same.
b. Some stars are closer to the Earth than others.
c. The light from some stars takes billions of years to arrive on the Earth.
d. Many different cultures are compelled to connect individual stars to others and form constellations.

19. Which of the following statements best captures the meaning of the final paragraph?

a. The Big Dipper can be difficult to recognize.
b. The Big Dipper is easy to see because it stays in the sky all night long.
c. The Big Dipper is special because it is not always easy to see.
d. The Big Dipper is easy to see because it contains the brightest stars in the night sky.

20. *Beowulf* is an epic poem that is important because it is often viewed as the first significant work of English literature. Although it was first written in AD 700, it is thought to be even hundreds of years older than that. It is believed that the story of *Beowulf* was told for centuries before it ever made its way on to paper. It is still taught today in various schools and universities.

***Beowulf* is a significant poem because:**

a. It was first written down in AD 700.
b. It was told for centuries before it was written down.
c. It is still taught today in academic settings.
d. It is the first important work of English literature.

21. At one time, people who wanted to be writers had to write a query letter to a magazine and then wait weeks, sometimes months, for a response, which was usually a rejection. Today, with blogs, virtually anybody can put their work out there for others to view. It's as easy as setting up your blog, naming it, and posting anything you want: opinions, poems, short stories, news articles, etc. Of course, while people who have blogs may choose to call themselves writers or journalists, it's unlikely they are making a living by putting their random thoughts out there into cyberspace.

It can be concluded that:

a. It is easier to make a living as a writer now.
b. There are more people who want to be writers now.
c. Most people do not submit query letters to magazines anymore.
d. There is no approval process for getting a blog.

22. A teacher wants to explain to her English class how to avoid plagiarism when writing an assignment. What should the teacher suggest that would BEST help to avoid plagiarism?

a. Rewrite information from research materials significantly.
b. Copy word-for-word and give attribution to research sources.
c. Copy word-for-word to be accurate.
d. Rewrite and give attribution to research sources.

23. What is true about teaching ESL students English-language reading, including alphabetic knowledge?

a. Formal instruction in a second language can accelerate students' acquisition of English.
b. Teachers should require ESL students to master each curriculum element consecutively.
c. Providing students with linguistic activities meaningful to them promotes ESL acquisition.
d. Letter-to-sound correspondences are the same across languages, so they transfer easily.

24. Abi, a fifth-grader, is reading aloud to his teacher during one-on-one reading time. His teacher uses this time to evaluate ongoing fluency and comprehension skills. Following today's reading, Abi's teacher determines that he needs practice with words that begin with digraphs. Which of the following sets of words would most likely be part of this assignment?

a. Chicken, Shells, That
b. Were, Frame, Click
c. Sponge, Think, Blank
d. Packed, Blistered, Smoothed

25. Which choice describes an appropriate alternative to round robin reading?

a. All students read together, simultaneously speaking the text aloud.
b. Students break into pairs assigned by the teacher to take turns reading the text while the teacher circulates among the pairs to guide and assess the students.
c. The teacher reads aloud to the students before engaging in a class discussion about what they have learned.
d. Students work on independent assignments while the teacher listens to students read individually.

26. At the beginning of each month, Mr. Yi has Jade read a page or two from a book she hasn't seen before. He notes the total number of words in the section and the number of times she leaves out or misreads a word. If Jade reads the passage with less than 3% error, Mr. Yi is satisfied that Jade is:

a. Reading with full comprehension
b. Probably bored and should try a more difficult book
c. Reading at her independent reading level
d. Comfortable with the syntactical meaning

27. An English teacher asked the students to research the literary and rhetorical terms listed on the table, show examples from literature, and have a class discussion about the meanings of the terms.

Literary and Rhetorical Terms

Allegory	Onomatopoeia
Alliteration	Oxymoron
Analogy	Paradox
Epigraph	Symbol
Hyperbole	Theme

The teacher's intent in having students research these terms would be to

a. familiarize them with these literary and rhetorical terms.
b. show the variety of language and style used in writing.
c. generate interest in reading diverse materials.
d. all of the above.

28. The teacher asked the students to keep a log of their summer reading. Lee kept the following log of his first book.

Title/Author	Genre	Goal	Personal Challenge Level 1-10 Explain	Did I accomplish my goal?
The Legacy of Bletchley Park by Annie Laura Smith	Historical Fiction	I wanted to read a book that explained codebreaking during World War II.	Level 5: I had trouble understanding why codebreaking was so complex.	Yes, Gretchen's fluent German helped her to translate the decoded messages. Her participation at Bletchley Park showed me the codebreaking process.

Which of the following literary strengths does Lee demonstrate in this entry?

a. an understanding of plotting techniques used in this story
b. an awareness of the value of conflict in this story
c. an interest in what is involved in codebreaking in this story
d. an awareness of character development in this story

29. A high school class reads an essay about the possible effects of sexual activity on teens. The author's position is very clear: she believes young people should avoid sex because they aren't mature enough to take the necessary steps to remain safe. The author cites facts, research studies, and statistics to strengthen her position. This type of writing is called:

a. Expository
b. Narrative
c. Persuasive
d. Didactic

30. The second graders are confused. They've learned to hear and count syllables. They understand that contractions such as *won't, didn't,* and *we're* represent two words converted into one. Now the teacher is trying to explain compound words. She has shown the children that a compound word is made of two words and has a meaning that is a little different from either of words that compose it. She pronounces *doghouse*, and asks if it is one word or two. "Two," the students correctly respond. The teacher now says *parent.* Again, the students tell her it's two words. The teacher explains there are two syllables but not two words. One child nods and says, "Like the word 'didn't.' That's two words but it sounds like one." What is the best way for the teacher to correct the students' misunderstanding?

a. Point out compound words the children use throughout the day. Write them on the board, and ask students to list them in their writing journals.
b. Assess the degree of confusion. Give the students a quiz listing a number of two-syllable words, compound words, and contractions. Ask the students to cross out the two-syllable words and contractions.
c. Write a compound word such as doghouse on the board. Underline dog, and then house. Beneath the words draw a picture of a dog and a house, joined with a plus sign. Next, write another compound word and ask the class to draw the pictures in their journals. Give the students a handout with several compound words. Ask them to underline the two words, then to draw the pictures.
d. Turn the lesson into fun by suggesting the students invent new compound words. Demonstrate by inventing one such as nosemitten instead of scarf. Children learn more readily when they are enjoying it.

Mathematics

31. In 1999, an office supply store sold 14,000 pens. In 2009, it sold only 12,600 pens. By what percent did the store's pen sales decrease from 1999 to 2009?

a. 1%
b. 5%
c. 10%
d. 15%

32. 30% of 50 equals 50% of what number?

a. 30
b. 25
c. 20
d. 15

33. If the average of 7 and x is equal to the average of 9, 4, and x, what is the value of x?

a. $x = 4$
b. $x = 5$
c. $x = 6$
d. $x = 7$

34. If four friends had an average score of 92 on a test, what was Annie's score if Bill got an 86, Clive got a 98 and Demetrius got a 90?

a. 88
b. 90
c. 92
d. 94

35. If 3x – 2 = 1, then x =

a. 4
b. 3
c. 2
d. 1

36. If a restaurant's salad dressing is made of a ratio of ¾ cup oil to ¼ cup vinegar, how many cups of vinegar are there in 6 cups of salad dressing?

a. ½
b. 1 ½
c. 1 ¾
d. 2 ¼

37. If $2^4 = 4^x$, then $x =$

a. 2
b. 4
c. 6
d. 8

38. If 2x + 3y = 13 and 4x – y = 5, then 3x + 2y =

a. 2
b. 3
c. 6
d. 12

39. A rectangle is divided into two squares, each with a perimeter of 20. What is the perimeter of the rectangle?

a. 20
b. 30
c. 40
d. 50

40. For what real number x is it true that $3(2x - 10) = x$?

a. -6
b. -5
c. 5
d. 6

41. A two-digit number is chosen at random. What is the probability that the chosen number is a multiple of 7?

a. $\frac{1}{10}$
b. $\frac{1}{9}$
c. $\frac{11}{90}$
d. $\frac{13}{90}$

42. If the ratio of the measures of the three angles in a triangle are 2 : 6 : 10, what is the actual measure of the smallest angle?

a. 20 degrees
b. 40 degrees
c. 60 degrees
d. 80 degrees

43. Henry is three times as old as Truman. Two years ago, Henry was five times as old as Truman. How old is Henry now?

a. 4
b. 8
c. 12
d. 16

44. If $a = 3$ and $b = -2$, what is the value of $a^2 + 3ab - b^2$?

a. 5
b. -13
c. -4
d. -20

45. Factor the following expression: $x^2 + x - 12$

a. $(x - 4)(x + 4)$
b. $(x - 2)(x + 6)$
c. $(x + 6)(x - 2)$
d. $(x + 4)(x - 3)$

46. The average of six numbers is 4. If the average of two of those numbers is 2, what is the average of the other four numbers?

a. 5
b. 6
c. 7
d. 8

47. How many 3-inch segments can a 4.5-yard line be divided into?

a. 15
b. 45
c. 54
d. 64

48. If a = 4, b = 3, and c = 1, then $\frac{a(b-c)}{b(a+b+c)}$ =

a. 4/13
b. 1/3
c. 1/4
d. 1/6

49. A student is asked to find the mode of the following set: {2, 4, 5, 6, 6, 7}.

The student's answer is 5. What has the student most likely done wrong?

a. The student has excluded the greatest and least values in the set.
b. The student has included both sixes in his calculation.
c. The student has found the mean instead of the mode.
d. The student has found the median instead of the mode.

50. Students are asked to convert 3/5 into a decimal. What is one possible first step?

a. Multiply numerator and denominator by two
b. Divide denominator by numerator
c. Multiply numerator by denominator
d. Raise denominator to the third power

51. 5(2 + 4) ÷ 2 = ?

A student composes the number sentence above in response to the following problem:
"Divide the sum of the products of 5 and 2 and 5 and 4 by 2."

How else could the student have written this number sentence?

a. 2 ÷ 5 × 2 + 5 × 4 = ?
b. 5 + 2 × 5 + 4 ÷ 4 = ?
c. [5(2) + 5(4)] ÷ 2 = ?
d. 5 + 2 × 5 + 4 ÷ 2 = ?

52. Students are given the following word problem:

"A jar of marbles contains six white marbles, eight black marbles, ten red marbles, and twelve green marbles. If John reaches into the jar and selects a marble, what are his chances of selecting a black one?"

Which of the following indicates a correct strategy for solving this problem?

a. 8^4
b. (6 + 8 + 10 + 12)/8
c. 8(6 + 10 +12)
d. 8/(6 + 8 + 10 + 12)

53. Students are given the following problem: $4a - 3 = 17$. What should their first step be?

a. Dividing both sides of the equation by four
b. Subtracting seventeen from both sides of the equation
c. Multiplying both sides of the equation by four
d. Adding three to both sides of the equation

54. Students are asked to find the sum of the following set: 3, 5.67, 40.54, and 1.765. What precaution should students make when performing this calculation?

a. Students should arrange the problem vertically, such that the decimal points are aligned.
b. Students should round all of the terms to the tenths place.
c. Students should ignore the decimal points in the terms and add a decimal point to the sum.
d. Students should only add two terms at a time.

55. Students are given the following word problem:

> "Andrea buys a shirt that is normally $24 but is being sold at a 20% discount. If Andrea pays a 5% sales tax on the shirt, what is the total cost?"

Identify the equation students should devise to solve this problem.

a. $24 \times 1.2 \times 0.05$
b. $[24 - (24 \times 0.2)] \times 1.05$
c. $24 \times 0.2 \times 0.05$
d. $24 - (24 \times 0.2) \times 1.05$

56. Students are asked to convert 5 2/7 into an improper fraction. Which operations will they need to perform?

a. Multiplication and division
b. Multiplication and addition
c. Division and subtraction
d. Division and addition

57. A student is presented with the following problem: $2(5 + 2) - 7^2 + 20$. Following order of operations, which operation(s) must the student perform before squaring seven?

a. Multiply two across the parentheses
b. Add the terms in parentheses
c. Both A and B
d. Neither A nor B

58. A student is asked to find the area of a triangle with a base of 5 and a height of 6. The student's answer is 30. What has the student most likely done wrong?

a. Nothing: the student's answer is correct.
b. Failed to multiply the product of 5 and 6 by 3
c. Failed to multiply the product of 5 and 6 by 1/2
d. Failed to multiply the product of 5 and 6 by 2

59. Students are given the following word problem:

"Vince asks for half of the remaining third of the peach pie. How much of a whole pie does Vince want?"

Which operation will students use to solve this problem?

a. Multiplication
b. Division
c. Addition
d. Subtraction

60. Students are asked to solve the following problem:

"Multiply the quotient of 6 and 2 by 4."

A student comes up with the incorrect answer of 48. What is the most likely cause of the student's error?

a. The student does not know the multiplication tables.
b. The student does not know the order of operations.
c. The student does not know the meaning of quotient.
d. The student does not know how to read.

Writing

Refer to the following for questions 61–63:

Picking the Perfect Pet

A

(1) Today's choices for pets go beyond the question of whether to get a cat or a dog? (2) Gerbils, rabbits, and amphibians is all popular options. (3) Before heading to an animal shelter, you need to know what pet makes sense for your home or classroom. (4) An obvious question to answer if you rent is if pets are permitted. (5) Some apartment complex places weight and size limits on pets or charge fees. (6) After gaining permission from the manager, your pet needs to be considered for other issues.

B

(7) If allergies effect someone in your home, be sure to select a pet that will not aggravate the condition. (8) Some dog breeds like the schnauzer and the poodle are acceptable pets for those who are sensitive to fur and dander.

C

(9) Irregardless of the pet you choose, think about other costs such as veterinary care and vaccinations, food costs, licensing, and equipment. (10) Does the pet need a special kind of home? (11) Who will be responsible for feeding and cleaning up after

the animal? (12) Taking time to do a little research can save you a lot of heartache and expense later.

61. Consider the following excerpt from the passage.

Sentence 1: "Today's choices for pets go beyond the question of whether to get a cat or a dog?"

Which change should be made to the selection?

a. NO CHANGE
b. change Today's to Todays
c. change question to questions
d. change the question mark to a period

62. What correction should be made to sentence (2)?

a. remove the comma after Gerbils
b. change amphibians to amfibians
c. change is to are
d. change Gerbils to Hamsters

63. Consider the following excerpt from the passage.

Sentence 5: "Some apartment complex places weight and size limits on pets or charge fees."

Select the best version of the underlined portion.

a. NO CHANGE
b. Some apartment complex places wait
c. Some apartment complexes places weight
d. Some apartment complexes place weight

64. Consider the following sentence:

If he stops to consider the ramifications of this decision, it is probable that he will rethink his original decision a while longer.

Select the best version of the underlined portion.

a. NO CHANGE
b. he will rethink his original decision over again.
c. he probably will rethink his original decision.
d. he will most likely rethink his original decision for a bit.

65. Consider the following sentence:

"When you get older," she said "you will no doubt understand what I mean."

Select the best version of the underlined portion.

a. older," she said "you will no doubt
b. older" she said "you will no doubt
c. older," she said, "you will no doubt
d. older," she said "you will not

66. Consider the following sentence:

Dr. Anderson strolled past the nurses, examining a bottle of pills.

Select the best version of the sentence.

a. NO CHANGE
b. Dr. Anderson strolled past the nurses examining a bottle of pills.
c. Dr. Anderson strolled past, the nurses examining a bottle of pills.
d. Examining a bottle of pills, Dr. Anderson strolled past the nurses.

67. Consider the following sentence:

Karl and Henry <u>raced to the reservoir, climbed the ladder, and then they dove into</u> the cool water.

Select the best version of the underlined portion.

a. NO CHANGE
b. first raced to the reservoir, climbed the ladder, and then they dove into
c. raced to the reservoir, they climbed the ladder, and then they dove into
d. raced to the reservoir, climbed the ladder, and dove into

68. Because land is limited and the population is constantly growing, real estate ________ typically ________ over time.

a. development ... falters
b. values ... increase
c. brokers ... compromise
d. agents ... magnify

69. Infants and toddlers may sometimes have ______ sleep patterns due to growth spurts and rapid changes in their physical development.

a. cohesive
b. natural
c. erratic
d. fanciful

70. The maintenance workers handle quite a range of ________: irrigation repair, plumbing, and general maintenance.

a. visitors
b. flowers
c. attractions
d. responsibilities

71. Natural fibers like organic cotton and bamboo are ______ and ______ without the use of harsh chemicals.

a. manufactured ... deployed
b. woven ... filtered
c. commissioned ... forgotten
d. grown ... processed

72. ________ mattresses contain many toxic substances, such as flame-retardants, adhesives and chemical foams, which are not present in natural latex rubber.

a. Conventional
b. Queen-sized
c. White
d. Maximum

Refer to the following for question 73:

Picking the Perfect Pet

(1) Today's choices for pets go beyond the question of whether to get a cat or a dog? (2) Gerbils, rabbits, and amphibians is all popular options. (3) Before heading to an animal shelter, it is important to know what pet makes sense for your home or classroom. (4) An obvious question to answer if you rent is if pets are permitted. (5) Some apartment complex places weight and size limits on pets or charge fees. (6) If pets are permitted, more issues need to be considered.

73. If sentence (6) was revised to begin with "<u>More issues need to be considered,</u>" the next words should be

a. permitted pets
b. if permitted
c. are permitted
d. if pets

Refer to the following for questions 74–75:

Fifteenth Birthday Parties

By Juan

(1) Last October, my sister turned fifteen. (2) When a girl turns fifteen where I am from (Mexico), her family has a big party for her and gives her a bunch of really nice presents. (3) My sister got some fancy jewelry and a new purse. (4) It was a nice day so we had the party under this really nice tent in the park. (5) All of my relatives came, even some that live really far away. (6) It was really nice of them to come. (7) When the party was almost over my sister was sort of sad because she knew that she would only have one party like this, but she was also really happy that all of the friends and family she loved were able to come.

74. What would be a better title for this essay?

a. "Birthday Parties in Mexico"
b. "A Family Holiday"
c. "My Sister's Fifteenth Birthday Party"
d. "Last October, My Sister Turned Fifteen"

75. What is one stylistic change the student might want to make?

a. The student should tell the story from the perspective of his sister.
b. The student should describe the presents in more detail.
c. The student should get a direct quote from his sister.
d. The student should use the word *really* less often.

Refer to the following for questions 76–77:

My Favrit Day

By Tom

(1) My favret day and I wak up in my bed and go to the kichen an my mem has mad some pancaks. (2) I relly luv these pancaks thet my mom maks and she knows how to mak them the best way. (3) When I go otside all my frens is there and we rid biks around the blokc and then go over the park and paly basketbal. (4) This is my favrit day but yurs mite be diffrnet. (5) When I go hom later my dad is ther and we throw around the ball and go ot fer ice cream.

76. Which is the best version of sentence (1)?

a. It's my favorite day, and I wake up in my bed and go to the kitchen to eat my mom's pancakes.
b. I eat my mom's pancakes in the kitchen after I get out of bed on my favorite day.
c. My favorite day begins when I wake up in my bed and go to the kitchen to eat the pancakes my mom has made.
d. My favorite day begins in the kitchen with mom's pancakes.

77. Which two sentences should be switched to improve this essay?

a. (1) and (2)
b. (4) and (5)
c. (2) and (4)
d. (1) and (3)

78. A student's paper contains the following sentence:

Each of the players picked up their bronze trophy after winning the championship game.

The student has made an error of

a. punctuation.
b. spelling.
c. grammar.
d. diction.

79. A student's paper contains the following sentence:

Denise told us not to wait, which she said would put us behind schedule.

What must the student do to correct this sentence?

a. Substitute *a mistake that* for *which.*
b. Substitute that for which.
c. Eliminate the comma.
d. Correct the spelling of *schedule.*

80. A student's essay contains the following passage:

"After we went back into the kitchen, Mom told me the truth. Couldn't believe it, and I had to run upstairs and get my yearbook to check."

What is wrong with this passage as written?

a. The second sentence is a run-on.
b. The second sentence is a fragment.
c. Yearbook should be two words.
d. *Mom* should not be capitalized.

81. Which word is NOT spelled correctly?

a. parallel
b. abscence
c. receive
d. principle

82. A student's essay contains the following sentence:

Football players spend a great deal of time looking at video, it helps them prepare for the upcoming opponent.

What could the student do to correct this sentence?

a. Place a hyphen in up-coming.
b. Divide it into two sentences.
c. Place an apostrophe in player's.
d. Nothing, the sentence is correct as written.

83. Students are asked to write a letter to the newspaper editor. What word best describes the appropriate tone for this letter?

a. measured
b. amusing
c. concerned
d. cynical

84. A student's paper contains the following sentence:

Performers of this day in age know the truth: making a living in show business is tough.

The student has made an error of

a. punctuation.
b. spelling.
c. grammar.
d. diction.

85. A student's essay contains the following sentence:

I don't know any teachers that would allow such behavior.

What must the student do to correct this sentence?

a. Substitute who for that.
b. Place a comma after teachers.
c. Substitute didn't for don't.
d. Eliminate the word *any*.

Refer to the following for questions 86–90:

(1) Passports, internationally, are recognized travel documents that verify their bearers' identity and nationality. (2) A valid US passport is required to enter and leave foreign countries. (3) The only authority to grant issue or verify United States passports is the United States Department of State (DOS). (4) And it does so through the Passport Services Office. (5) This office of the DOS: Bureau of Consular Affairs (CA) provides information and services to American citizens about obtaining, replacing, renewing or correcting/changing a passport.

(6) You are required to apply in person at any of the over 9,000 passport acceptance facilities located throughout the United States to obtain a passport for the first time. (7) You must provide certain supporting documents and two recent photographs of yourself when you apply or renew. (8) Application forms can be completed online using the Passport Application Wizard, but must be printed prior to submission.

(9) The United States issues both traditional passport books and limited use passport card. (10) You may obtain either one or both of these, depending on your travel needs. (11) Additional information for passports, including answers to frequently asked questions, is available through the DOS: National Passport Information Center (NPIC).

86. Which is the best version of sentence 1?

a. NO CHANGE
b. Passports are recognized documents, internationally, that verify their bearers' identity and nationality.
c. Passports are internationally recognized travel documents that verify their bearers' identity and nationality.
d. Internationally, passports are recognized travel documents that verify its bearers' identity and nationality.

87. Consider the following excerpt from the passage.

Sentence 3: The only authority to grant issue or verify United States passports is the United States Department of State (DOS).

Select the best version of the underlined portion.

a. NO CHANGE
b. The only authority to grant, issue or verify United States passports
c. The only authority to grant, issue, or verify United States Passports
d. The only authority to grant, issue, or verify United States passports

88. Consider the following excerpt from the passage.

Sentences 3–4: The only authority to grant issue or verify United States passports <u>is the United States Department of State (DOS). And it does so through the Passport Services Office.</u>

Select the best version of the underlined portion.

a. NO CHANGE
b. is the United States Department of State (DOS): and it does so through the Passport Services Office.
c. is the United States Department of State (DOS); and it does so through the Passport Services Office.
d. is the United States Department of State (DOS), and it does so through the Passport Services Office.

89. Which is the best version of sentence 6?

a. NO CHANGE
b. To obtain a passport for the first time you are required to apply in person at any of the over 9,000 passport acceptance facilities located throughout the United States.
c. To obtain a passport for the first time, you are required to apply in person at any of the over 9,000 passport acceptance facilities located throughout the United States.
d. You are required to apply in person, at any of the over 9,000 passport acceptance facilities located throughout the United States, to obtain a passport for the first time.

90. What is the best version of sentence 9?

a. NO CHANGE
b. The United States issues both traditional passport books and limited use passport cards.
c. The United States issue both traditional passport books and limited use passports card.
d. The United States issues both traditional passport books and limited use's passport card.

Answer Key and Explanations for Test #2

Reading

1. A: Technical passages focus on presenting specific information and have a tone of formality. They also usually prompt a response from their recipient. Expository passages reveal information to the reader. This passage does give information, but the information is specific, technical, and meant to prompt action from the students receiving the email. Therefore, technical (A) is the best answer. Narrative writing focuses on telling a story, and the passage offers no indication of this. Persuasive writing attempts to persuade the reader to agree with a certain position; the instructor offers the students information and advice but leaves the decision up to each student.

2. B: This question asks for the best summary of the instructor's motive. In the opening paragraph, the instructor notes that his original grading plan has to change to reflect the exam scores. Because they were low, he now wants to give students a chance to make up for their low scores. Choice B thus summarizes his motive effectively by stating that he recognizes the need for a change in the policy. The instructor introduces his email with the notes about the scores being posted, but given the information that is provided in the message, this is not the sole motive for his writing, so choice A is incorrect. Choice C limits the motive to the details about the group project, but the instructor provides three options. Choice D overlooks the instructor's further note about how the grading policy sometimes has to bend to reflect circumstances.

3. D: The professor is designing the project in option one, so this project is guaranteed to be an acceptable alternative to the essay exam. The professor encourages students to choose this option, as the other two options may not yield projects that are acceptable alternatives. If students choose options two or three, there is a chance they may not be eligible for the entire 150% of the point value the professor is offering. The professor states that there will be no additional extra credit opportunities and emphasizes that each student may only choose one extra-credit option, so choices A and B are incorrect. Option three states that each student will receive equal credit, but it does not state that the 150% of the point value will be divided among the students, so choice C is incorrect.

4. C: The sentence reads, "Your brain <u>filters</u> [your nose] out," which means your brain ignores it.

5. B: Only choice B reflects the meaning of the term "retina," which is a part of the eye's anatomy.

6. B: The final sentence reads, "Your brain works hard to make the world look continuous." It follows that visual perception is an active process, not a passive one, making choice B the best answer.

7. A: If the reader follows the instructions given in the paragraph, the O and X in the middle of the passage can be used to demonstrate the blind spot in the visual field.

8. B: The passage explains the way that visual perception works.

9. D: Much of the information in the passage is provided to show examples of how the brain fills in gaps in the visual field.

10. A: The author of the passage mentions the nose to demonstrate how the brain filters information out of the visual field.

11. B: Choice B can be inferred from the second paragraph. The paragraph states that the brain filters out information, which means that the brain does not perceive all activity in the visual field.

12. B: The meaning of this term can be found in the context of the sentence. Choice B, "stays in the sky all night," is closest in meaning to the statement "so it can be seen all night long."

13. D: This passage's purpose is to inform the reader of different interpretations of this group of stars.

14. A: Only choice A can be correctly inferred from the third paragraph.

15. C: Only choice C is consistent with the meaning of the passage.

16. C: Choice C is closest to the meaning of the passage.

17. C: Choice C best captures the way the passage uses the term <u>code</u>.

18. D: Though several of these statements are true, only choice D is directly related to the passage itself.

19. B: Choice B best captures the meaning of the final paragraph.

20. D: The passage directly states that *Beowulf* is important because "it is often viewed as the first significant work of English literature," making D the correct answer choice.

21. D: This can be concluded based on the section of the passage that states "Today, with blogs, virtually anybody can put their work out there for others to view. It's as easy as setting up your blog, naming it, and posting anything you want."

22. D: Rewriting significantly and giving attribution to research sources will avoid plagiarism. A is incorrect because rewriting significantly is only part of the answer. B is incorrect because giving attribution to the sources is only part of the answer. C is incorrect because copying word-for-word without attribution is plagiarism and would not be advised.

23. C: When teachers provide language-related activities for ESL students that are relevant to them personally, this is found to help them acquire English. Formal instruction does NOT speed up English acquisition (A): it can facilitate and inform the process and expand ESL students' knowledge, but because language learning is not linear, formal instruction will not make it happen faster. For this reason, teachers also should NOT require ESL students to master every individual curriculum element before starting another (B). Teachers must also realize that letter-sound correspondences are NOT the same across languages (D). For example, Spanish letters correspond better to their sounds than in English; therefore, native Spanish speakers are apt to be confused at the multiple sounds of many English letters/letter combinations (e.g., "-ough" as in *through, though, rough, ought, bough*).

24. A: It is important to evaluate specific reading skills, such as phonemic awareness, in a variety of contexts. Reading aloud with Abi allowed his teacher to notice that he consistently misread words beginning with digraphs. Digraphs are sounds in which two distinct letters, when combined, produce a single third sound (e.g., when *s* and *h* produce the *-sh* sound). Blends are words in which two letters produce a third sound which is a combination of both sounds put together (e.g., *b* and *l* combined to make *b*). The only set of words consisting only of digraphs is choice A.

25. B: The intention of round robin reading is to provide practice reading aloud with appropriate fluency. This practice is also used to cover a large quantity of text with the entire class during the class period. By pairing the students, each child will get more practice reading aloud. He or she will also be more likely to stay engaged when working with only one partner, as there will be less time and fewer opportunities to become distracted. The teacher can then circulate amongst the groups to encourage focus and concentration, as well as provide guidance on fluency and comprehension of the text. As long as the students are paired carefully, this strategy is most likely preferable to the round robin method.

26. C: When reading independently, students are at the correct level if they read with at least 97% accuracy.

27. D: Such an assignment would align with a goal to familiarize students with these literary and rhetorical terms, show the variety of language and style used in writing, and generate interest in reading diverse materials.

28. C: It shows his interest in codebreaking. A is incorrect because it is not his interest in plotting. B is incorrect because it is not his interest in conflict. D is incorrect because it does not show his interest in characterization.

29. C: The author is hoping to persuade or convince young readers to avoid sex by providing them with facts and using rhetorical devices, such as dispelling opposing arguments.

30. C: Write a compound word such as *doghouse* on the board. Underline *dog,* and then *house.* Beneath the words draw a picture of a dog and a house, joined with a plus sign. Next, write another compound word and ask the class to draw the pictures in their journals. Give the students a handout with several compound words. Ask them to underline the two words, then to draw the pictures. Students will discover that compound words are composed of two distinct words that in combination mean something new but related.

Mathematics

31. C: The decrease was the difference between 14,000 and 12,600: 1400. 1400 is 10% of 14,000.

32. A: 30% of 50 is determined by multiplying 30/100 x 50. The answer is 15. Then, we need to find the number that 15 is 50% (or ½) of. This can be found by using the equation 15 = 1/2x. x = 30.

33. B: The average of 7 and x is $\frac{7+x}{2}$. The average of 9, 4, and x is $\frac{9+4+x}{3}$.

$$\frac{7+x}{2}=\frac{13+x}{3}$$

To solve, start by cross-multiplying.

$$3(7+x)=2(13+x)$$

Then, distribute and solve for x.

$$21 + 3x = 26 + 2x$$
$$3x = 5 + 2x$$
$$x = 5$$

34. D: This is a simple average problem. If x denotes Annie's score, then $\frac{86+98+90+x}{4} = 92$. Now, multiply both sides by 4 and solve for x:

$$86 + 98 + 90 + x = 368$$
$$274 + x = 368$$
$$x = 94$$

35. D: If 3x - 2 = 1, then 3x = 3. Therefore, x = 1.

36. B: Determine what the ratio of vinegar to the salad dressing as a whole is. Vinegar is ¼ of a cup and the salad dressing as a whole is ¼ cup vinegar plus ¾ cup oil, or 1 cup. Thus, vinegar is ¼ of the salad dressing. Therefore, ¼ of 6 cups is 3/2 or 1 ½ cups of vinegar.

37. A: Follow the rules of exponents: $2^4 = 2 \times 2 \times 2 \times 2 = 16$. Therefore, $4^x = 16$; $x = 2$.

38. D: Solving for y in the second equation gives y = 4x-5. If we plug this into the first equation we get 2x + 3(4x-5) = 13. Solving for this equation gives us 14x = 28, or x = 2. Then, plug the value of x into either equation to solve for y. y = 3. Therefore, 3x + 2y = 12.

39. B: The perimeter of a square is four times the length of any one of its sides. If a square's perimeter is 20, the length of any side is 5. The perimeter of this rectangle is six times the length of a side, which is 30.

40. D: To solve 3(2x – 10) = x, first multiply the left side out. 6x – 30 = x. Therefore, 5x = 30, and x = 6.

41. D: There are 90 two-digit numbers (all integers from, and including, 10 to 99). Of those, there are 13 multiples of 7: 14, 21, 28, 35, 42, 49, 56, 63, 70, 77, 84, 91, 98. Therefore, the probability of choosing a number that is a multiple of 7 is $\frac{13}{90}$.

42. A: The sum of the measures of the three angles of any triangle is 180 degrees. The equation for the sum of the angles of this triangle can be written as $2x + 6x + 10x = 180$, or $18x = 180$. Therefore, $x = 10$. We multiply 2 by 10 to find that the measure of the smallest angle is 20 degrees.

43. C: If t equals Truman's age now, and 3t equals Henry's age now, t-2 equals Truman's age two years ago and 3t-2 equals Henry's age two years ago. Since Henry was 5 times as old as Truman two years ago, we can solve for 3t–2 = 5(t-2). Solving this gives us 3t-2 = 5t-10 or 2t = 8. Therefore, t = 4. Since Henry is three times as old as Truman, Henry is 12.

44. B: Substitute the given values for a and b into the expression.

$$a^2 + 3ab - b^2$$

$$(3)^2 + 3(3)(-2) - (-2)^2$$

From here, simplify the expression using the order of operations.

$$9 + 3(3)(-2) - 4$$

$$9 + 9(-2) - 4$$

$$9 - 18 - 4$$

$$-9 - 4$$

$$-13$$

Therefore, the value of the expression is −13.

45. D: To solve this problem, work backwards. That is, perform FOIL on each answer choice until you derive the original expression.

46. A: A set of six numbers with an average of 4 must have a collective sum of 24 because $6 \times 4 = 24$. The two numbers that average 2 will add up to 4 ($2 \times 2 = 4$), so the remaining numbers must add up to 20 ($24 - 4 = 20$). The average of these four numbers can be calculated by dividing the sum by the amount of numbers: $20 \div 4 = 5$. Therefore, the average of the other four numbers is 5.

47. C: For this problem there are 3 inches in each segment, 12 inches in a foot, and 3 feet in a yard. Set up a conversion problem and simplify.

$$4.5\ \cancel{\text{yd}} \times \frac{3\ \cancel{\text{ft}}}{1\ \cancel{\text{yd}}} \times \frac{12\ \cancel{\text{in}}}{1\ \cancel{\text{ft}}} \times \frac{1\text{ segment}}{\cancel{3\ \text{in}}} = 4.5 \times 12\text{ segments} = 54\text{ segments}$$

Therefore, a 4.5-yard line can be divided into 54 3-inch segments.

48. B: Substitute the given values and solve. Resolve the parenthetical operations first.

49. C: The student has found the mean instead of the mode. The mean, or average, is the sum of the terms in the set divided by the number of terms. In this case, that calculation would look like this: (2 + 4 + 5 + 6 + 6 + 7) ÷ 6 = 5. The mode, however, is the term used most often in a number set. In this set, 6 is the only number that appears more than once and is therefore the mode.

50. A: One possible first step for this problem would be to multiply the numerator and denominator by two. A fraction can be easily converted into a decimal if the denominator ends in a power of ten. Since the denominator of 3/5 is five, multiplying both numerator and denominator will yield an equivalent fraction of 6/10, or six tenths. This is easily converted into the decimal 0.6. The more traditional method for converting a fraction into a decimal is to divide the numerator by the denominator (the opposite of the operation described in answer choice B).

51. C: The student could have also composed his number sentence as 5(2) + 5(4) ÷ 2 = ? According to the distributive property of multiplication, 5(2 + 4) = 5 × 2 + 5 × 4. Remember that many problems can be arranged correctly as several different number sentences. The important consideration is to arrange the number sentence such that it will be performed in the proper order. In this problem, the sequence should be multiplication, addition, division.

52. D: The expression 8/(6 + 8 + 10 + 12) indicates a good strategy for solving this problem. The word problem asks students to determine the probability of finding a black marble in a jar containing several different colors of marble. The best way to find the answer is to set up a fraction with the number of black marbles in the numerator and the total number of marbles in the denominator. This fraction will look like answer choice D. The expression simplifies to 8/36 = 2/9, meaning that there is a 2 in 9 chance of selecting a black marble.

53. D: The student's first step should be adding three to both sides of the equation. Solving a simple algebraic equation of this type requires isolating the variable on one side. This process could begin by dividing each side by four (thus eliminating the coefficient from $4a$), but this would be much more complicated than simply adding three to both sides. Students should be trained to resolve this type of equation in the easiest way possible. Adding three to both sides yields an equation of $4a = 20$, which, once both sides are divided by four, leaves $a = 5$.

54. A: When performing this calculation, students should arrange the terms vertically, such that the decimal points are aligned. It is easy for students to get confused when performing addition or subtraction with groups of numbers that have varying amounts of digits to the right of the decimal point. The best way to arrange such a problem is vertically. Students will also find it easier to perform this calculation if they add zeroes where necessary to give each number the same length to the right of the decimal point. In this problem, then, the terms would become 3.000, 5.670, 40.540, and 1.765.

55. B: Students should use the equation $[24 - (24 \times 0.2)] \times 1.05$ to solve this problem. The problem requires students to calculate the sale price of the shirt and then add the sales tax. The discounted price is calculated by subtracting the amount of the discount (24×0.2) from the original price of the shirt (24). This operation is placed in brackets so that it will be completed before moving on to the second part of the problem, adding the sales tax. The sales tax is described as 5%, which is expressed as a decimal 0.05. However, the total price will include the discounted shirt price as well as 5% of that price in sales tax, so the total price must be calculated by multiplying the discounted price of the shirt by 1.05.

56. B: Students will need to perform multiplication and addition in order to convert 5 2/7 into an improper fraction. Converting a mixed number into an improper fraction is a relatively simple operation. The whole number, five in this case, is multiplied by the denominator (seven). The product (35) is then added to the numerator, yielding an improper fraction of 37/7. A fraction is described as improper when the numerator is larger than the denominator.

57. B: The student must first add the terms in the parentheses before squaring seven. This problem requires knowledge of the order of operations: operations inside the parentheses, exponents, multiplication and division from left to right, addition and subtraction from left to right. Some students may find it easier to remember the order of operations using a mnemonic like "Please Excuse My Dear Aunt Sally," in which the first letters of the words are the same as for the operations. While it is possible to achieve the correct solution by multiplying the two across the parentheses before squaring the seven, this does not follow order of operations, and it will not always work out that way.

58. C: The student has most likely failed to multiply the product of 5 and 6 by 1/2. The equation for finding the area of a triangle is $A = 1/2bh$. It appears that the student has multiplied the base and height of this triangle but has neglected to multiply by 1/2.

59. A: Students will use multiplication to solve this problem. This word problem requires students to perform fraction multiplication. Vince wants 1/2 of 1/3, which can be calculated $1/2 \times 1/3 = 1/6$. The answer, then, is that Vince wants 1/6 of a whole pie. Remember that the multiplication of fractions does not require a common denominator.

60. C: The most likely cause of the student's error is that she does not know the meaning of *quotient*. A student would arrive at the incorrect answer of 48 if she multiplied 6, 2, and 4. This is most likely the student's mistake. A quotient is the answer to a division problem. The quotient of 6 and 2 is 3, which multiplied by 4 yields the correct answer of 12.

Writing

61. D: The sentence is declarative, not interrogative. So, the sentence needs a period as the end mark. Choice B is not correct because the apostrophe is needed to show possession. Choice C is incorrect because it does not solve the problem, and it creates a problem of agreement. Choice A is incorrect as well. The reason is that the sentence has an error that needs to be corrected.

62. C: The sentence contains a disagreement between the compound subject, which is considered plural, and the singular verb. Changing *is* to *are* solves the problem. Choice A is incorrect; the comma is needed for items in a series. Choice B is not correct; the word is correctly spelled as written. Choice D, likewise, is incorrect; it offers only a cosmetic change, not a solution to the problem of subject-verb agreement.

63. D: The problem in the sentence as written is one of subject-verb agreement and colloquial or substandard English. *Some* indicates that more than one apartment complex is being discussed. It, therefore, is necessary to change both the subject and verb to plural. Choice A is incorrect; the sentence as written clearly contains an error to be remedied. Choice B is incorrect; choosing an alternative spelling for the homonym does not solve the problem. Choice C is incorrect as well; it creates a different subject-verb agreement problem.

64. C: The original sentence is redundant and wordy.

65. C: The syntax of the original sentence is fine, but a comma after "said" and before the open-quotation mark is required. Choice C is the only one that includes this comma.

66. D: In the original sentence, the modifier is placed too far away from the word it modifies.

67. D: The verb structure should be consistent in a sentence with parallel structures.

68. B: The word "because" at the beginning of the sentence indicates that a reason is being given for the condition described in the second clause. Answer B logically completes the sentence: increasing demand for a limited resource leads to an increase in its value.

69. C: The second part of the sentence suggests that growth spurts and rapid physical changes disturb sleep patterns, so they are not likely to be "natural." Of the remaining choices, only "erratic" makes sense, and it provides a good description of a disturbed pattern.

70. D: The list that follows clearly describes tasks for which maintenance workers may be responsible as part of their jobs.

71. D: The sentence describes the advantages of natural organic fibers for the consumer. Choice D describes the steps required to bring them to market.

72. A: The sentence contrasts the properties of typical, or "conventional", mattresses with natural ones. The properties listed obviously have no connection with mattress size or color.

73. D: The question tests students on sentence reconstruction, placing the independent clause, rather than the dependent clause, first. The first words of the dependent clause, *if pets*, must, therefore, come first. Choice A is incorrect; building a phrase around these two words is grammatically impossible. Choice B is also not correct; one cannot create a clause from such a beginning. Option C is incorrect as well; beginning with the verb is not a good choice.

74. C: "My Sister's Fifteenth Birthday Party" would be a better title for this essay. The student's title, "Fifteenth Birthday Parties," is much too vague and gives the impression that the essay will be about these special parties in general, when in fact it is about one party in particular. A title should be as specific as possible without failing to encompass every part of the text. The other answer choices are either too vague (A and B) or specific (D).

75. D: The student should use the word *really* less often. This word is used five times in the essay. Like *very* and *pretty*, *really* is intended to add emphasis but is too vague and bland. It should be used rarely except in direct quotation, since it is a common conversational placeholder. Students should be taught to weigh the value of each word in their writing, and to eliminate those words that take up space without adding meaning.

76. C: A better way of phrasing the first sentence would be, "My favorite day begins when I wake up in my bed and go to the kitchen to eat the pancakes my mom has made." This corrected sentence is still a bit long, but it at least divides the thoughts grammatically. Answer choice A is a run-on sentence. Answer choices B and D give the impression that the student is taking pancakes away from his mother rather than eating pancakes prepared for him by her.

77. B: Sentences (4) and (5) should be switched to improve this essay. The fourth sentence, though quite ungrammatical, is a general statement that would be more effective as a summary at the end of the passage. The fifth sentence, on the other hand, continues the sequence of events as they were described.

78. C: The student has made an error of grammar. The subject of the sentence is the singular *each*, so the plural possessive pronoun *their* is incorrect. Instead, the student should substitute *his*, *her*, or *his or her*. This is a common error in writing and speech.

79. A: To correct this sentence, the student must substitute *a mistake that* for *which*. As originally written, the sentence has an unclear pronoun. It is difficult to determine the reference for *which*. Making the recommended substitution clarifies the sentence.

80. B: The second sentence of this passage is a fragment. It may seem strange to call this sentence a fragment, since it includes both subjects and verbs, but it does have a subject in the initial clause. The sentence would be correct if written, "I couldn't believe it, and I had to run upstairs and get my yearbook to check." *Yearbook* is always one word, and *Mom* should be capitalized when it is being used as a proper noun (that is, in place of a name). If the student had written "my mom," it would be appropriate to leave the pronoun in lowercase.

81. B: The word *abscence* is not spelled correctly. The correct spelling is *absence*. Paraprofessionals should know the commonly misspelled words. *Receive* obeys the frequently cited rule of spelling: "*i* before *e* except after *c*." *Principle* is spelled correctly, though there is also a homophone (word that sounds the same), *principal*. A *principle* is a belief or tenet, while a *principal* is the head of a school.

82. B: To correct this sentence, the student could divide it into two sentences. As written, this is a run-on sentence because it contains two independent clauses without a conjunction between them. One way to correct this sentence would be to substitute a period or semicolon for the comma. Another would be to substitute the word *because*.

83. A: A letter to the newspaper editor should have a measured tone. The audience for a letter to the newspaper editor is presumably educated and literate, but its opinion about a particular issue would be hard to guess. For this reason, the most effective letters to the editor are those that sound calm and reasonable. A typical newspaper reader will be put off by a letter that sounds cynical, and attempts at humor may be inappropriate.

84. D: The student has made an error of diction. The phrase *day in age* is commonly, and incorrectly, used in place of *day and age*. This phrase is conversational rather than formal, though, and should be avoided. Diction is word usage. The sentence is otherwise correct. A colon is appropriate for presenting an independent clause in this manner.

85. A: To correct this sentence, the student must substitute *who* for *that*. This is a common mistake for writers and speakers at all levels. People should always be referred to with the relative pronoun *who* or *whom*. This is true even when the antecedent of the pronoun is a job title, as in this sentence. The relative pronouns *that* and *which* are used to refer to non-persons. Writers are given some freedom with regard to animals. Depending on the context, animals may be assigned any of the relative pronouns.

86. C: The adverb *internationally* modifies the adjective *recognized*. Therefore, choice C has the best grammar and flow. Choice A has *internationally* incorrectly modifying *passports*. Choice B misplaces the adverb *internationally* after the word *documents*. Choice D has a singular pronoun modifying a plural noun.

87. D: Choice D has the necessary commas. Choice A is lacking commas after *grant* and *issue*. Choice B needs an additional comma after *issue*. Choice C incorrectly capitalizes *passports*.

88. D: The sentences should be joined by a comma to make one sentence, which choice D does. Choice A is wrong because there are two sentences, but the word *and* indicates a continuation of the idea. Choice B incorrectly uses a colon. A semicolon is used when there are two independent ideas, which is not the case in choice C.

89. C: The sentence in choice C flows better than the other choices and correctly uses a comma for an interrupter. Choice A does not flow. Choice B lacks the necessary comma. Choice D is not corrected by adding commas and still reads poorly.

90. B: Choice B is correct because both *books* and *cards* should be plural. Choice A lacks the plural *cards*. Choice C is incorrect because the verb *issue* is in the plural form rather than the singular form. Choice D is incorrect because there is no reason for the word *use* to be in a possessive form.